Soul Analysis

What your Birthday Reveals about your Spiritual Destiny

Chavah Aima

Copyright © 2014 by Chavah Aima

All rights reserved. No part of this book may be reproduced or transmitted in any form or by any means, electronic or mechanical, including photocopying, recording or by any information storage and retrieval system, without permission in writing from the Publisher. Reviewers may quote brief passages.

Enlightened Life Publishing
3801 North Capital of Texas Hwy, E240-633
Austin, Texas 78748
U.S.A.
www.enlightenedlife.org

ISBN: 978-0-9705518-3-2

Book design, layout and cover by
Sel P (sel.designroom@gmail.com)

Printed in the U.S.A. by Lightning Source, Inc.

The information contained in this book is derived from ancient wisdom sources and is for spiritual purposes only. There are a multitude of factors that can influence the psychological, emotional or mental development of any profile. You are responsible for your life and well-being, and how you choose to apply the information contained in this book. Neither the publisher nor the author shall be liable or responsible for any problems allegedly arising from any information in this book.

TABLE OF CONTENTS

ACKNOWLEDGEMENTS   v

INTRODUCTION   1

SOUL ANALYSIS PROFILE DIRECTORY   5

CHAPTER 1: THE SOUL ANALYSIS PROFILE: SPIRIT, SOUL & PERSONALITY   11

CHAPTER 2: THE PROFILES OF THE WILLFUL CONSCIOUSNESS   31

CHAPTER 3: THE PROFILES OF THE INTUITIVE CONSCIOUSNESS   63

CHAPTER 4: THE PROFILES OF THE INTELLECTUAL CONSCIOUSNESS   95

CHAPTER 5: THE PROFILES OF THE WORLDLY CONSCIOUSNESS   131

ACKNOWLEDGEMENTS

The beginning and completion of this work would not have been possible without the manuscript known as *Book T* produced by 'S Rioghail Ma Dhream, MacGregor Mathers, in the late 1800's. His keen insights and brilliant illumination of the mysteries of the Universe provided the framework upon which Soul Analysis is built. Though *Book T* is cryptic, and the notes it contains are brief and were applied primarily to the interpretation of the Tarot cards for the past 120 years, this material stimulated my quest to discover the higher purpose of the planetary, numerological and other symbolism it revealed.

I am deeply grateful to 'S Rioghail Ma Dhream for his inspired vision of humanity as a spiritual race, and indebted to his scholarship and erudition. During the 18 years I worked on this project to expand upon his original concepts and redefine them into the form of spiritual psychology I have called Soul Analysis, I felt his presence often as an encouraging, guiding light. As he wrote at the end of *Book T*, I also - *have not only transcribed the symbolism, but have tested, studied, compared and examined it both clairvoyantly and in other ways. The result of these has been to show me how absolutely correct the symbolism of the Book T is, and how exactly it represents the occult Forces of the Universe.*

In the process of creating Soul Analysis and developing an accurate understanding of the universal forces that comprise each profile, I was also assisted by the work of the great Western adept and disciple of Sri Ramana Maharshi, Mouni Saddhu. His unusual book, *The Tarot*, found its way to me during a magical journey to Glastonbury, England. I had long meditated on the symbolism involved in these archaic systems and prayed many times for additional knowledge to come to me. In response to these heartfelt desires, I suddenly found myself in a small metaphysical bookstore, holding this treasure of wisdom in my hands. Used and somewhat battered, its transcendental content nevertheless activated additional critical insights that spurred me onward in the journey to unveil the mysteries of the soul. My gratitude and appreciation for the wisdom of Mouni Saddhu is immeasurable.

Finally, without the hundreds of people who have sought me out over the years to receive their Soul Analysis profiles, this book would not be possible. Each person who sat with me for their profile reading provided validation when my instincts were correct and essential feedback that helped eliminate erroneous presumptions. Additionally, their presence with me allowed me to enhance my intuitive perceptions of each profile and clarify all of the subtleties they imply. I extend heartfelt thanks to each and every one of you. This book is the result of your willingness to discover a greater truth about yourself, your loved ones and friends and go beyond the limitations of human understanding.

INTRODUCTION

The most important discovery that we can make in life is the realization that we are spiritual beings, not merely humans alternately aspiring and struggling through life. To get in touch with our spiritual nature is the greatest blessing on earth. When we do so, we can transcend limitations and gain a deeper understanding about the nature of our worldly lives. Soul Analysis is a system of spiritual psychology that reveals the spiritual beings we truly are. Its insights give meaning to our existence, shift our identity from the personal to the soul and bring us into alignment with our spiritual mission and destiny.

Soul Analysis comes from an ancient tradition of ageless wisdom that draws from astrology, numerology, the Tree of Life and other metaphysical philosophies that offer a holistic, spiritual perspective on human psychology. This book provides highlights of each profile in the Soul Analysis system. While these key points are inspiring and informative, more detailed information on the origin, symbolism and applications of Soul Analysis can be found in the *Practitioner's Companion Guide: Unlocking the Secrets of Soul Analysis,* a resource book provided to Soul Analysts as a part of their certification program.

The *Practitioner's Companion Guide* assists counselors, psychologists, mentors and coaches – and anyone who wants to help others realize their full potential - to master the Soul Analysis method. Soul Analysis is an insightful tool that allows us to understand the nature of the spiritual influences that are active throughout the universe on each day of the year. These energies create distinctive souls and form each individual's human personality. A certified Soul Analyst can help you learn a great deal more about your personal profile, show you how to master all of your important relationships and guide you to fulfill your spiritual mission.

With the Soul Analysis profile, we can understand the spiritual consciousness, soul mission and personal strengths and challenges of any individual based on their date of birth. In the 18+ years I have been working with this approach to self-awareness and personal discovery, I have repeatedly seen how the powerful revelations found within each Soul Analysis profile can profoundly awaken and transform my clients and change the course of their lives.

The secrets of this timeless system, which allow us to see deeply into the spirit, soul and personality, required many years to decipher and master. As a result, when I created Soul Analysis, I wanted to make these life-changing insights easy for anyone to access and understand. This book will allow you to look up a synopsis of your profile and those of your friends, loved ones and co-workers. This information helps us begin to realize that there is far more to this human life that we so often take for granted. There is a wise Soul watching over this identity we call the personality and our spiritual destiny can be known.

May your profile ignite your soul's passion, lead you into a life of greater love, understanding and happiness, awaken you to the vision of who you really are and help you master all that you came into this life to do.

Chavah Aima
April, 2014
Austin, Texas
U.S.A.

SOUL ANALYSIS PROFILE DIRECTORY

IDENTIFY THE SPIRIT, SOUL AND PERSONALITY PROFILES BY FINDING THE BIRTH DATE IN EACH OF THE 3 DATE RANGES THAT INCLUDE THAT DATE.

DATES	PROFILE	PAGE
June 21 to September 22	Spirit: Willful Consciousness	31
June 21 to July 11	Soul: Intuitive Visionary	35
June 21 to July 1	Personality: 2 of Intuition	38
July 2 to 11	Personality: 3 of Intuition	40
July 12 to August 11	Soul: Willful Mediator	42
July 12 to 21	Personality: 4 of Intuition	44
July 22 to August 1	Personality: 5 of Will	46

August 2 to 11	Personality: 6 of Will	48
August 12 to September 11	Soul: Worldly Warrior	50
August 12 to 22	Personality: 7 of Will	52
August 23 to September 1	Personality: 8 of World	54
September 2 to 11	Personality: 9 of World	56
September 12 to 22	Soul: Intellectual Visionary	58
September 12 to 22	Personality: 10 of World	60
September 23 to December 21	Spirit: Intuitive Consciousness	63
September 23 to October 12	Soul: Intellectual Visionary	67
September 23 to October 2	Personality: 2 of Intellect	69
October 3 to 12	Personality: 3 of Intellect	71
October 13 to November 12	Soul: Intuitive Mediator	73
October 13 to 22	Personality: 4 of Intellect	75

October 23 to November 1	Personality: 5 of Intuition	77
November 2 to 12	Personality: 6 of Intuition	79
November 13 to December 12	Soul: Willful Warrior	81
November 13 to 22	Personality: 7 of Intuition	83
November 23 to December 2	Personality: 8 of Will	85
December 3 to 12	Personality: 9 of Will	88
December 13 to 21	Soul: Worldly Visionary	90
December 13 to 21	Personality: 10 of Will	92
December 22 to March 20	Spirit: Intellectual Consciousness	95
December 22 to January 9	Soul: Worldly Visionary	99
December 22 to 30	Personality: 2 of World	101
December 31 to January 9	Personality: 3 of World	103
January 10 to February 8	Soul: Intellectual Mediator	105

SOUL ANALYSIS PROFILE DIRECTORY

January 10 to 19	Personality: 4 of World	108
January 20 to 29	Personality: 5 of Intellect	110
January 30 to February 8	Personality: 6 of Intellect	112
February 9 to March 10	Soul: Intuitive Warrior	114
February 9 to 18	Personality: 7 of Intellect	117
February 19 to 28	Personality: 8 of Intuition	120
March 1 to 10	Personality: 9 of Intuition	122
March 11 to 20	Soul: Willful Visionary	125
March 11 to 20	Personality: 10 of Intuition	128
March 21 to June 20	Spirit: Worldly Consciousness	131
March 21 to April 10	Soul: Willful Visionary	134
March 21 to 30	Personality: 2 of Will	137
March 31 to April 10	Personality: 3 of Will	140

April 11 to May 10	Soul: Worldly Mediator	143
April 11 to 20	Personality: 4 of Will	145
April 21 to 30	Personality: 5 of World	148
May 1 to 10	Personality: 6 of World	151
May 11 to June 10	Soul: Intellectual Warrior	154
May 11 to 20	Personality: 7 of World	157
May 21 to 31	Personality: 8 of Intellect	160
June 1 to 10	Personality: 9 of Intellect	163
June 11 to 20	Soul: Intuitive Visionary	166
June 11 to 20	Personality: 10 of Intellect	169

Chapter 1

THE SOUL ANALYSIS PROFILE: SPIRIT, SOUL & PERSONALITY

To locate and read your personal Soul Analysis profile, go to the profile directory on page 5, look up your birth date and turn to the pages listed. This chapter contains additional important information about the four types of consciousness, the three soul types and the numerology of the personalities that you will also want to read to learn more about your profile.

In the Soul Analysis system, each individual profile includes a spirit, soul and personality. There are four spirit types, reflecting the four primary kinds of consciousness that we see in every profile. There are three basic types of souls and nine personality types that are defined by numerology as well as their associated consciousness. In the sections below you will learn more about the interpretation of these factors that are found in every profile. Taking time to review this information will help you get the most from your Soul Analysis.

Soul Analysis reveals your spiritual destiny

Soul Analysis is a system for understanding spiritual energy, the mission of the soul and the personal challenges and rewards we experience in life. It is a tool for personal growth and discovery that can help awaken our awareness of the higher purposes of life. It has commonality with astrology and numerology, but informs us that the planets, zodiac signs and numbers connected to our date of birth were selected by the spirit, which is our true identity.

Soul Analysis invites you to consider yourself in a far greater way than perhaps you ever have, to see yourself as a soul with an important spiritual destiny to be carried out through a specific personality type. You are not only the personality, with its particular characteristics conditioned by the influence of the planets, zodiac signs and numbers that were dominant in the universe on the day you were born. Soul Analysis consistently identifies and describes you from a completely spiritual point of view.

Soul Analysis tells us that each human is a spiritual being with special qualities, gifts, challenges and potentials that are designed to accomplish a spiritual mission in life. The specific nature of these qualities is discerned by the date of birth. Each profile reveals the primary consciousness of the spirit, the mission of the soul and the tendencies, talents and struggles of the personality. No two people who have the same profile will experience themselves in exactly the same way, but the overall themes described by the profile will generally be present. Life takes many twists and turns, and is always subject to change. Yet, the imprint of spirit's intention motivates the soul, which guides and supports the personality through the ups and downs of life.

Spirit

There are four spirit types, each representing the pure form of one of the four kinds of consciousness – willful, intuitive, intellectual and worldly – which are found throughout the Soul Analysis system. These four modes of consciousness are also present in every soul and personality type. Individuals can have a combination of various types of consciousness in their profile. For example, the birthdate may place the spirit within the intellectual consciousness, the soul may be of the willful type and the personality may be intuitive. In some cases the spirit, soul and personality are all of the same type of consciousness. These four forces of consciousness are explained in detail at the beginning the following chapters where you will find complete descriptions of each spirit type. These same descriptions always apply to the four types of consciousness that are assigned to the soul and personality types as well.

Spirit is your essential nature – an individual expression of divine consciousness. It is free-flowing and unconditioned. Spirit can be thought of as the God-self, the part of you that is completely divine and beyond the limitations of the soul's karma and the personality's likes and dislikes. Pure consciousness is the Absolute, Supreme Being or Creator. This absolute, unified consciousness divides itself into four distinct expressions: *willful, intuitive, intellectual and worldly*. These separate streams of consciousness have particular qualities that will be expressed in life. The consciousness type assigned to the spirit is pure and unconditioned. When it is found within souls or personalities it is somewhat modified, based upon the soul's type and personality numbers. Spirit type is based upon the season of the year in which you were born.

Soul

There are three primary soul types in the Soul Analysis system: Warrior, Visionary and Mediator. The soul types are influenced by numerology and each one is associated to a particular number. In some cases, the soul and personality have the same number. When this occurs, it indicates closeness between the soul and personality that isn't found in many of profiles. The number of the soul and personality and the difference between them is one of the factors considered in analyzing the profile. For example, the Warrior is aligned with the number 2, but works with personalities numbered 7, 8 and 9, which indicates these individuals experience a feeling of distance between the soul and personality. Whereas the Mediator, whose number is 6, partners with personalities numbered 4, 5 and 6, which indicates less distance between the soul and the personality.

Each soul also incorporates one of the four types of consciousness. For example, the Warrior soul type may be Willful, Intuitive, Intellectual or Worldly, depending on the date of birth. This makes a total of 12 soul types, which are discussed in depth throughout the chapters that follow. Below are the general meanings of the three primary types of soul.

Warrior

The Warriors are the oldest souls, having had many previous incarnations. Warriors are associated to the number 2, and in addition to their other characteristics, they express the qualities of this numerology, which are detailed in the personality section below. Willpower is their primary characteristic as well as their individual challenge. They are intensely focused on their mission in life. They may seem aloof or distant in some way because their spiritual energy is elevated and the soul is at home on the celestial plane. Because of their many lifetimes, they often take on difficult challenges in life. This struggle is required for the Warrior to grow in wisdom, because they have already been through many battles in past incarnations before coming into this life.

They have deep wisdom, which is beyond words and language. They can spontaneously recognize the deeper meanings of symbols, geometrical patterns and mathematical formulas. They instinctively understand the rhythms of human life and the nature of spiritual things, but they cannot easily share their inner knowing verbally with others. This can lead to feelings of isolation, though many of them embrace their solitude and independence. They are determined and ambitious and prefer to work alone.

Warriors are mature souls who work through some of the most demanding and intense personality types. There is some distance between the soul and its various personalities, which involves a divide between the spiritual and material worlds. The Warrior is courageous and well-equipped for the task of synthesizing these two diverse realms. They have a definite spiritual mission in life, which relates directly to the type of consciousness they hold. The mission of each type of Warrior is highlighted in the following chapters.

Warriors are capable of tremendous spiritual insight. They seek mastery over the material world in order to continue to expand themselves into divine consciousness. The paradoxical nature of the interactions that occur between the Warrior and the various personalities provides abundant opportunities to elevate and transcend the allures of sensuality, the limitations of the lower mind and the illusions of the dualistic world. They have the armor of wisdom to protect them and spiritual light to guide them on the path as they seek to gain and share enduring wisdom. The Warrior realizes that the battles of life must be fought and won in order to win the victory for spirit. The Warrior souls embody the personality types numbered 7, 8 and 9.

Visionary

The powerful and mysterious Visionaries are intuitive, sensitive and commanding. Their imaginative nature heightens their creativity. Visionaries are associated to the number 3, and in addition to their other characteristics, they express the qualities of this numerology, which are detailed in the personality section below. They receive visions and often have gifts of clairvoyance, mysticism and telepathy. They have a deep understanding of the mysteries of life and are motivated by a profound compassion. The Visionaries are highly intelligent, well-spoken and aware. Like the Warriors they have access to deep wisdom within; but the Visionaries are able to give words to this subtle knowledge and share it in fresh, original ways.

They are generally confident, noble and kind. They are perceptive and impressionable, sensing the moods and intentions that lie beneath words. They can unconsciously take on negative energy from others and their surrounding environment. They hold onto these things and their own feelings as well, and their soul's journey is designed to show them how to let it all go. This tendency toward holding is reflected in their affinity for baskets, bags and containers of all kinds.

Visionaries are typically considerate and helpful. They freely share their many insights, intuitions and advice. They have a tendency to insist they know best with loved ones and friends, and they can be overbearing even though their intention is to assist. They are good directors, managers and overseers because they are able to absorb a great deal of information without ever losing track of the big picture. They are commanding when they lead, and their certainty and charm draws others to follow their suggestions.

Their emotional responses are acute and they may be moody at times. They are highly sensitive in every way, even if they do not appear to be so from the outside. Their senses are keen and their feelings are intense. They are driven by the deep impulses of the celestial plane and always do better when they follow their inner knowing. In love, they are generous and passionate, and they may have many intimate encounters and relationships in their lives.

They may feel alone and misunderstood by the world. This is due to the elevated nature of this soul type and its natural perceptive and visionary state. They have the ability to understand others and the world itself. They may be saddened by the seeming inability of others to grasp the subtle nature of their soul, but need to remember that the calling of the Visionary soul is to bring greater understanding into the world. They are not here to be understood, but to understand.

The Visionary soul is paired with personality types numbered 2, 3 and 10. Because of this, the Visionaries have rulership over the last personality profile within each spirit type and the first two profiles of the next spirit type. This is why the description for each visionary is given near the end of each chapter along with the entry for the personalities numbered ten, and repeated in conjunction with the personalities numbered two and three at the beginning of each chapter.

Mediator

Mediators are the youngest souls, though they have lived many lives and have a wealth of knowledge to share. Mediators are associated to the number 6, and in addition to their other characteristics, they express the qualities of this numerology, which are detailed in the personality section below. They are tremendously intellectual and receive mental stimulation through inspired ideals. They find creative ways to bring their interior illuminations into the world to refine, revolutionize and uplift human life. Enthusiastic, exuberant and social, they weave connections between the spiritual and material planes, and between people and groups.

As the name of the soul indicates, they are superb mediators, being gifted in negotiation and reconciliation. They can be headstrong, because they have seemingly endless energy and determination. Mediators are talented, talkative and entertaining. They are most at home in the center of a group of family, friends or colleagues. They like to take the lead in organizing, managing or arranging the details for work-related tasks and social or family activities.

Mediators are incredibly busy in their personal, career and daily lives. They are typically surrounded by calendars, schedules and agendas because they have a variety of special interests to which they devote their time. They are also good at managing hectic household routines on behalf of their family members, keeping everyone motivated, on track and on time. While they are genuinely aware of the needs of others, their self-focus is strong as well. They have an appealing air of celebrity about them and a need to be recognized and acknowledged for the many gifts they bring.

They prefer peaceful environments and cooperative people. In spite of this, they often find themselves involved in resolving disputes, clarifying confusion and moderating arguments. To bring order out of chaos and heal misunderstandings is the mission of this soul, which is why they are inevitably called upon to referee, counsel and consult. This calling also aids the soul to grow in patience, acceptance and love.

Mediators are sensitive and intuitive, although they spend time reasoning out the significance of the inner promptings they receive. They boldly express their opinions once they have organized these insights into beliefs. In love, they help their mates to realize their greater potential by encouraging an orderly approach to self-development. They are spirited coaches who promote lifestyles and interests that contribute to the improvement of life. Though they are sensual and affectionate, they sometimes hesitate to fully explore the power of their sexuality. They are here to learn to equilibrate energy in the body, the mind and the world. The Mediator soul works with personality types numbered 4, 5 and 6.

Personality Numbers

In the Soul Analysis system, the consciousness of spirit motivates a specialized soul to master life's lessons in harmony with one of 36 personality types. The personality is a unique vehicle built by spirit to carry the soul through life. It is a collection of specific characteristics that will contribute to or obstruct the mission of the soul, depending upon its overall disposition. Each personality type is associated with one of the four types of consciousness. They are further distinguished by the numbers two through ten. For example, a personality type is titled 2 of Will, 3 of Intuition, 4 of Intellect, 5 of World, and so on. The personality number is an important element in analyzing the nature of each type. Below are the primary meanings of the personality numbers.

2

Twos have wisdom that is beyond language and words. They have a deep, inner knowing that guides them in life. They are strongly oriented toward love, relationships and partnerships. Twos are generally balanced and have a special harmony within them. While generally passive, a two will typically advocate for the restoration of peace even in adversarial situations. They are emotional, sensitive, adaptable and intuitive – and are often psychic and able to pick up on the thoughts and feelings of others.

Twos are compassionate and loving, and generally slow to anger. When they do express their unhappiness they typically bring up past incidents that hurt them, though they didn't react to them at the time. They have good memories and are excellent communicators, but they tend to be quite serious and need to remember to lighten up and enjoy life. They usually have several important love relationships throughout their lives.

Twos spend a great deal of their lives trying to find the perfect mate, but due to their great patience and idealistic dreams, they may stay involved too long in relationships that are not good for them. Their sexual energy is generally quite high and this drives their quest for intimate partners, but they can lack discernment in regard to sexual encounters, though this usually improves as they grow and mature. In work they enjoy their independence although they can work with a partner successfully as well. Cooperative, considerate and harmonious, these individuals love to serve others and have many spiritual gifts to share.

3

Threes are capable of understanding and explaining just about anything. They are excellent communicators. Family is a key focus for them and they are lifelong, loyal friends. Threes are charismatic and attractive, having a good sense of humor that helps them succeed in life. They are outgoing, active and organized. They tend to be somewhat emotionally unstable due to their great sensitivity toward others and life. They are naturally spiritual, and this potential is best developed through structured and organized means such as religion, churches or traditional systems.

They are emotional and empathic, and may react strongly to the pain and suffering of others, but they often suppress these strong emotions because of a need for stability and to feel in control. This tendency can tempt them to indulge in self-medication with alcohol or drugs.

Threes have many talents and creative gifts, and their overall attitude is childlike, enthusiastic and kind. However, they have to watch out for negativity and dark feelings that they may harbor at various times. A Three can be successful in almost any career as long as they find ways to express their strong leadership abilities and natural enthusiasm.

They enjoy flirtations and sexual encounters, but when they settle down with their beloved mate they are devoted and monogamous and committed for life. Threes make excellent parents who love to spend quality time with their children, helping them to learn and grow. They are usually blessed with a happy home and material success.

Orderly, organized and dependable, the Fours bring charisma and grace to the world. They are compassionate, kind and loving. Their creative intelligence helps them master all that life brings their way. Although they sometimes struggle and scrabble for success, their perseverance will usually bring rewards later in life. Loyal and hardworking, they may take on too much and suffer stresses and strains.

In general, they are grounded, stable, practical and logical – but they are also emotionally and psychically sensitive, and may have clairvoyant or visionary gifts. Fours are oriented toward service and assistance to others. Their passive nature may be a cause for concern as they can sometimes be vulnerable to experience deception, manipulation or abuse in relationships. They are natural caretakers who are influenced by the emotions and needs of those who surround them, but may lose track of their own identity and needs in the process of excessively caring for others.

Fours can be excellent advisors, counselors, healers and guides, but need to remember to take a break and spend some quality time with themselves as well. In love, they are gentle, devoted and sweet-natured. Their goodwill and generosity spring from the spiritual energy they carry within. They are inspired by the ideals of cooperation and peace.

Their ability to arrange thoughts, emotions, and matter into effective structures helps them keep their balance amid the chaos of the material plane. Learning to set and enforce reasonable personal boundaries enables these individuals to focus on contacting the higher energies of the soul. When they have achieved this soul communion they can serve as channels for the healing force of the divine and may establish enduring humanitarian works on earth.

Fives are righteous, willful and just. They encounter challenges in life related to tempering their personal will, recovering from losses and establishing enduring success. They are strong leaders and deep thinkers who take bold actions. Fives are productive and hard-working individuals who strive to maintain their independence. They can be dispassionate analyzers with a special ability to discern potential pitfalls, delays and deceptions. They may be prone to conflict because they tend to forcefully express their heartfelt views.

Fives are given opportunities to complete karmic lessons of all kinds, one of which is to redirect destructive powers into creative acts. They love the earth and nature, which reflects their own stability in the midst of volatile change. They are often agents for change on earth, and possess special gifts that purify, temper or disrupt in order to correct errors and imbalances. Fives are usually deliberate and focused in their thoughts and behaviors, though their emotions can be explosive. This is especially true when they feel frustrated or threatened.

Typical life lessons for fives include learning to be patient, silently tolerating imperfections and applying their courage and creativity in ways that serve others. They are serious in love and devoted to their lifelong mate, family and friends. They are sociable and outgoing, sensual and sexually energetic. They need to find an intimate partner whose sexuality is equally dynamic. They do well when they integrate spirituality into their lives, which nurtures the soul. An active spiritual practice or outlet for worship or faith can help them transmute personal will into a powerful spiritual force.

Six is the number of harmony, beauty and balance. The Sixes appreciate symmetry, equality and cooperation. They are devoted to reconciliation, mediation and the restoration and maintenance of peace and goodwill. Highly intelligent, active and youthful, they are generally successful on the material plane. They are tolerant, affectionate and accepting, and have a natural and spontaneous love that motivates and guides them through life. However, they cannot abide violence, ignorance or intolerance in others. They have a close affinity to the soul and are driven by this intimate connection.

Passionate and hard-working, they bring tremendous enthusiasm to everything they undertake. Sixes have a childlike innocence that is endearing, but may delay their emotional maturity. They are self-focused and self-aware, which typically gives them great self-confidence and a tendency toward bold or dramatic expressions. In love they are devoted mates and parents who seek to protect and provide for their family in the best possible way. Sixes are challenged to overcome and temper the ego, which allows them to better express the creative impulses of the soul.

They are innovators, entertainers and revolutionaries with a vision of perfection and the desire to see it come to life on the material plane. This can result in frustration because perfection is not possible on earth. As they mature, they realize that the imperfections they perceive are part of the natural process of evolution and change. Sixes want to bring a more unified awareness into the dualistic world to ease suffering, stimulate growth and awaken humankind. They are typically found engaged in endeavors that allow them to share their insights and talents with others. These individuals are providing an important link between the material and spiritual planes in service to the planet.

7

Sevens are sensual, artistic and wise. They are typically diligent and ambitious in attaining their many goals in life. Generally sweet-natured, loving and kind, they do not rely too much on the logical mind, but derive knowledge and understanding by intuitive means. Their strong passions and desires can lead them astray, but their inherent spiritual nature will normally help them get back on track. They are acutely sensitive to people and environments, and their emotional reactions can be intense. They prefer to dive deep into subjects that provoke their curiosity, mastering each topic before moving on.

Sevens are influenced by a powerful, dynamic and unpredictable force, the primal urges of nature in a raw and savage state. They feel this energy in a tangible, physical way, and may seek to express it rather dramatically. They are naturally drawn toward mystical states, but if they do not respond to this soul calling, the urge may devolve into the abusive use of intoxicants, sexuality and food. They are highly sexual and enjoy exploring diverse ways to experience this force. They can suffer emotional damage if restricted from expressing their erotic drives, which are directed more thoughtfully as they mature. This attraction to pleasure on the physical plane can lead them toward spiritual awakening, if they become involved in traditions that teach methods to exalt this energy into higher expressions.

They love the earth, their significant others, family and friends. They are oriented toward service to others, artistic works, healing professions and education. Sevens are old souls learning to command a great spiritual force within the world, and when they conquer their challenges, they can inspire, enlighten and lift up everyone whose lives are blessed by their unique presence.

Eights are orderly, intellectual and precise. They analyze, retain and draw upon a great wealth of information and knowledge that they acquire in life. Insightful and artistic, they appreciate beauty, harmony and the rhythms of life. Eights are thoughtful and use their strong minds to decipher life's mysteries. Sociable, family-oriented and dependable in work and in love, they make good managers due to their ability to track details and critique others' work.

Eights prefer to live life according to a set of deeply-held beliefs and need to remember to keep an open mind. Their logical impulses are typically automatic and operate outside of their conscious control. Their life lessons challenge them to develop balanced insights and a gentler approach to self-reflection. They tend to be critical of others and themselves because they have an inner vision of pure perfection that cannot truly be realized in the physical world. However, they can use their creativity to express the beauty they envision, and doing so helps them to gain greater intimacy with the soul.

Eights often face challenges in their emotional and physical health, which stems from over-reliance on their abundant intellectual skills. They are usually surrounded by a small group of friends, selectively choosing to spend their time with those whose values and beliefs are in harmony with their own. They are emotionally sensitive, but do not always have sufficient resources to cope with intense feelings. Eights are destined to learn to build trust, heal wounds and be vulnerable in love. They have access to a secret mysticism deep inside, and if they explore this potential, it can help them go beyond the restraints and limitations of the serious mind.

Nines are intuitive, psychic and visionary. They are often in touch with the invisible realms, spirit guides and loved ones who have passed on. They may experience precognition or prophetic dreams, which may be troubling to them when they are young. They need to develop their reason and logic to avoid delusions, nightmares and despair. They might sometimes use their powerful minds to deny and suppress their ethereal awareness, which would be a mistake as these insights can benefit them in important ways. Nines may also lack discernment when contemplating these visions, and act on them too quickly without really thinking it through.

They are sensual and appreciate the pleasures of the physical body and the world. They tend to be successful and materially sustained, and are equally driven in work and at play. Nines need to find the right partner for their journey through life, one who will appreciate their sensitive side, but also draw them out from their seriousness. They are trustworthy advisors and loyal friends, and are empathic toward all living things. Their emotional receptivity can cause moodiness and withdrawal. This time out helps them to regain their composure, but they should guard against brooding too long in isolation from others.

Nines are oriented toward service, advocacy and counseling. They can apply their intuition and intellect to resolve problems, mediate disputes and reconcile opposition. Their wisdom develops as they mature, and when they apply their spiritual gifts they bless others with insight, knowledge and love.

The Tens are usually fulfilled in their worldly lives. They have a deep connection to nature, the earth, the planets and stars, and are comfortable with all aspects of material life, the body, emotions and mind. They can be successful in business, real estate or finance. They are independent and prefer to focus their energy and attention on their own values and goals. Tens have an important mission in life, and once they realize their calling, they wholeheartedly commit to manifesting it on earth. In relationships, they prefer to take the lead, but their life's work typically remains their primary task.

Tens are naturally commanding, yet can become overly passive depending on their experiences in early childhood. If they suffer neglect, abuse or exploitation, they can struggle to cope with the emotional impact and spend the rest of their life trying to recover. This is because of their tendency to cling to the past and repeat dysfunctional patterns. It is possible for Tens to inflict damage on others instead of being subject to abuse themselves, as even without any history of emotional trauma, they can have an intense need to control that may lead to harsh or insensitive actions.

They embrace and love the physical world, and spending time outdoors is important to their health and wellbeing. They can be quite outspoken when their passion is aroused, and will defend or protect their zealous beliefs. They are loyal friends, but they are called to learn to let others direct and lead sometimes. It can be challenging for them to find the right mate in life as they need someone who is equally enthused about their life's mission and willing to help them fulfill it.

Tens are intelligent and intuitive, which helps them discern the true intentions of any person or the best response to any situation. Their highest calling is to establish a legacy that will benefit humanity and endure upon the earth. They do well when they get involved in a spiritual path, especially traditions related to nature and the cosmic rhythms of the universe.

Chapter 2

JUNE 21 TO SEPTEMBER 22

CANCER, LEO AND VIRGO

SPIRIT TYPE: WILLFUL CONSCIOUSNESS

Love in Action

KEYWORDS

WILL AMBITION INTUITION COMPASSION
UNDERSTANDING ANALYSIS LEADERSHIP
FAITH CREATIVITY

People born within the willful consciousness are driven by a power that lies beyond mind and words. They typically feel a strong sense of being on a mission; focusing their energy on manifesting a higher will on earth. Whether they are headstrong or passive, they are here to learn about will, and how to master this powerful force. Generally intuitive, they have a strong sense of being guided by energies deep within them that they cannot always express in language.

These spirits are among the most creative, passionate and determined individuals on earth. When they find their calling, they commit to it with strength, power, conviction and faith. They are commanding leaders and, though they can be team players, it is not easy for them to take direction from anyone else. They are often found working for themselves, which gives them the independence they need to achieve their destiny on earth.

Their energy comes and goes, and they can alternate between outward and inward moods. Emotions run deep among these fiery spirits, and they often feel compelled to listen to the voice within, even when engaged in relationships with others. They are equally immersed in an interior world of mysticism, and the exterior world where they seek to creatively transform themselves, others and life on earth. They take on many challenges in life, relying on spirit, willpower and love to see them through.

These spirits have the opportunity to learn how to ground powerful cosmic energy into the earth. The volatile forces they wield can be difficult to manage emotionally, mentally and physically. Though they are primarily adventurous and daring, their challenge is to use their dramatic tendencies in service to others. They are capable of intense focus, which helps them attain whatever they need to accomplish their dreams. Due to their great sensitivity, they may be acutely aware of the thoughts and emotions of others, so they benefit from developing appropriate boundaries.

Those born within the willful consciousness are not limited by the rational mind, and may not respond to overly structured mental concepts. They are guided in their decisions and actions by deep, intense impulses of a potent spiritual force. This strong drive may open them to greater spiritual awareness and stimulate dedication to humanitarian causes.

Their will is strong when activated, and even when they appear to be passive, they are still in touch with a mighty force that energizes and guides them at every moment. When they determine a course of action, they will pursue it with it with great intensity. They are not easily distracted or dissuaded from their path and can be quite intimidating toward anyone who gets in their way.

Their conviction that their approach is the right one may appear egotistical; however, it is actually derived from a much deeper level of consciousness. Nevertheless they need to learn when to apply their tenacious determination and fight for their heartfelt beliefs and when to let go and reserve their energy for more important battles. Their challenge is to develop the strength to follow their inner knowing while remembering to balance self-will with appropriate consideration of the needs of others.

Fortunately, in addition to their tremendous willpower, these spirits are loving, gracious, considerate and kind. They thrive on service to others, particularly when they can apply their considerable leadership skills. They are capable of seeing the big picture and keeping everyone's best interest in mind. Their point of view is often radical, encompassing leading-edge breakthroughs and revolutionary changes that can advance humankind.

Regardless of the nature of their worldly work on earth, they do well when they express themselves creatively. Whether through art, music, theater, writing or mysticism, their unique point of view will definitely attract attention. They may shift their attention from one expression to another throughout life because they are innovators, and when their work in one realm is complete, they will be compelled to move on and apply their fiery enthusiasm to initiate new, transformational ventures that progress and expand human understanding.

These spirits are here to increase their self-awareness, and need to recognize that the primal, unconditioned will that motivates them may be distorted by the personality into attention-seeking, self-absorption or domination. They are at their best when they share their abundant optimism, and make their strong will into good will by leading others toward greater compassion and providing for those in need.

The willful consciousness is a natural force that is spontaneous, derived from and motivated by love. These spirits must find a way to balance their boldness with compassion for others, and transform thrill-seeking into a quest for spiritual attainment. Though this powerful energy can result in forceful and direct expressions at times, these spirits are motivated by innocence rather than malice. The willful consciousness stimulates new beginnings, inspired knowledge and radical initiatives in the profiles under its influence. This spirit's highest potential is to embody unconditional love in every action and take time to give service to others.

JUNE 21 TO JULY 11
SOUL PROFILE: INTUITIVE VISIONARY

KEYWORDS

MYSTICAL   SENSITIVE   WISE   COMPASSIONATE
SPIRITUAL   NURTURING   EMPATHIC   EMOTIONAL

This soul's energy is derived from the feminine source, and is very nurturing, giving and creative. They are compassionate, concerned for others and focused on family. These souls tend to be organized, and create a sense of order in their environments. They like to keep everyone harmonious and happy. All of the Visionary soul types turn the wheel of the universe from one spirit type to the next. The Intuitive Visionary therefore oversees the last personality profile of the Worldly consciousness, and the first two personas of the Willful consciousness.

Their profound depth and understanding makes them not only sympathetic but acutely empathic. They tend to absorb feelings and energy from others and from their environment, and reflect it back to those around them. It is important for them to master this potentially healing gift, and not be disempowered by caretaking others or taking on too much negative energy.

Emotional, moody and very intense, the fire of willful consciousness illuminates these paradoxically placid souls, and gives them a strong psychic nature. They not only have deep knowledge, but are gifted with being able to explain the essence of this wisdom to others. They like to organize information and often learn or create systems that further human understanding. These souls are very interested in helping others in a wide variety of ways, including feeding, comforting, housing, nurturing, giving wisdom, inspiring, harmonizing and clarifying.

These individuals do best when they create ways to share their spiritual faith, heartfelt impressions, and intuitions with others in life. When the Intuitive Visionary sets out to assist others, they do so in a way that brings forth whatever may be lying beneath the surface, waiting to be seen and healed. These souls bring unique spiritual gifts to a world in which they are desperately needed; however, they often feel distant from the material world and more at home on the inner planes.

They carry a deep wisdom that manifests in unusual ways and they need to find outlets for their innovative understandings. They may feel isolated and misunderstood, which is very real because few can understand the mysterious ways of the Visionary soul. They can be passive at times, especially in relationships and they must learn to develop a stronger will to prevent others from taking advantage of them. They are highly receptive and easily pick up prevailing forces and passions from environments and people. They need to remember to consciously release these things in order to preserve their serenity and peace of mind.

They are highly compassionate and often seek ways to help improve the world. Their great sensitivity causes them to react strongly to the words and actions of others. Their memory is particular enduring and it takes a long time for them to forget wounding words. They not only hold onto the past, but to people and things as well, and are particularly fond of bowls, vases, boxes and bags, which symbolize containment.

Like all of the Visionaries, they are commanding and can easily oversee large projects, family matters and projects of all kinds. They are good at directing and encouraging the successful completion of any task because they see the big picture as well as intuiting the best application of the skills of each person involved. They need to be careful that their masterful oversight doesn't devolve into bossiness or control. They are here to learn to perfect the delicate balance between encouragement and dominion.

These souls are natural clairvoyants and rely upon their strong inner connections to guide them in life. If they choose to do so, they may be successful as spiritual advisors. At the least they will serve their family and friends with accurate insights and guidance. Their dreams may be precognitive and prophetic, and they may be aware of the invisible beings who are always present in the world. As children this can be difficult because they are typically unaware that not everyone shares this spiritual gift. As they mature, the resources they find to support their spiritual nature can range from charismatic churches to ritual lodges. One way or another they will be drawn to prayer, meditation and spiritual life.

These insightful individuals can be successful in a variety of ways. Counseling, creating or teaching are some of the outlets that can sustain them. In love they are tender, sensitive and sensual and they need a partner who appreciates their magical ways. As parents they are nurturing and committed to meeting their children's needs. They need to be careful of over-involvement and avoid smothering their loved ones by becoming entangled in their lives. When they learn to step back and allow others to learn from their struggles, they complete one of the most important goals of the soul.

The qualities of the Intuitive Visionary are absorbent, reflective and changeable, stimulating sensitivity, insight and healing for humankind. They are imaginative, creative, kind, nurturing and mystical. They are strong spiritual leaders once they have mastered their sensitive nature, and can benefit others by exposing them to the reality of the unseen, inner and spiritual aspects of life.

JUNE 21 TO JULY 1
PERSONALITY PROFILE: 2 OF INTUITION
Harmonious Love

KEYWORDS

COOPERATION　　LOVE　　PARTNERSHIPS　　FAMILY　　MYSTICISM
NURTURANCE　　COMPASSION　　EMPATHY

These affectionate individuals personify love and compassion. They are primarily gentle, kind and loving. With a natural charm that is attractive and magnetic, their strong sense of higher love motivates them to seek perfect balance in all of their personal and professional relationships. They are highly sensitive to the words and expressions of others, and maintain their serenity by withdrawing into themselves from time to time. However, they must be careful not to isolate loved ones by doing so. Peace and unity are essential in their environment, and they will do all they can to both maintain and restore harmony.

These people are highly sensitive and have an intense inner life. They are deeply connected to the spiritual energy of the soul, and often have a unique understanding of others. Their compassionate tendencies and superior spiritual knowledge may lead them into work that involves teaching, counselling and healing others. They benefit most from their great receptivity by turning toward spiritual life, delving into ancient wisdom and developing detachment in love. As they do so, they share the insights they have gained through wise counsel, empathic understanding and cooperative work.

These individuals are oriented toward love relationships, family and marriage. They may be actively involved in the lives and passions of their family members, and are often driven to find their true spiritual partner on earth. Consequently, they may have many relationships or marriages. In their careers, they are cooperative, but often find they do best when they can work independently.

They have an acute awareness of pain and suffering that may feel overwhelming at times, but they are challenged to transform their emotional responses to human tragedy and come to see divine love in every circumstance. As they mature, their deep empathy can lead to involvement in charitable and humanitarian acts. They tend to hold onto emotions and need to realize that the distress they feel may well have nothing to do with them. They are constantly absorbing energetic projections from others and over-stimulating environments. It is important for them to consciously release these things in order to restore their balance.

They spend a great deal of time searching for the right relationship and hold an inner vision of a perfect union that drives them in their quest. They will typically try to bring this ideal into reality, only to realize over and over the futility of their efforts. Their core lesson involves realizing that the only true harmony lies within and cannot be fully manifested in the outer world where perfection is an elusive dream. When they awaken to this truth, they can apply their visionary gifts toward developing a more realistic and enduring love.

Because they are benevolent and capable of great sympathy, they need to be aware that others might take advantage of their generous nature. These extraordinary visionaries may feel isolated by their unique inner understandings and natural connections to spiritual love. These individuals benefit greatly from strengthening their will to compliment their unrestrained compassion. Establishing self-discipline enables these individuals to set boundaries with others, and give more wisely.

JULY 2 TO JULY 11
PERSONALITY PROFILE: 3 OF INTUITION
Creative Abundance

KEYWORDS

SUCCESSFUL   FORTUNATE   FAMILY-FOCUSED
AUTHORITARIAN   COMMUNICATIVE   FAITHFUL
VOLATILE   SELFISH

These individuals strive to establish and maintain command in virtually every setting, and especially in their home environments. They appreciate order due to their detailed minds. They are usually quite busy as they are highly creative people who enjoy being of service to others. They have a natural affinity toward religion and spirituality, which can help them overcome selfish tendencies.

They have a special combination of intellect and imagination that stimulates them to create new technologies, organize information in innovative ways and make it accessible to others. Naturally creating abundance in every aspect of their lives, their positive energy gives them a joyful outlook, and they tend to be successful.

Due to their ability to see the big picture, they do well in careers that allow them to work for themselves or train and supervise others. They are able to track detailed information, analyse complex systems and keep others on track to accomplish tasks and goals. They can be good team players when they remember to let go of their need to control.

In love they are emotional, devoted and kind. They like to be in charge so it's wise for them to find a partner who values and supports their point of view. They are loyal provided their lover meets their extraordinary sensual needs. Great passion and intensity are integral to intimate life for these expressive individuals. Their feelings are easily hurt in spite of their somewhat dominant outer nature and they do best with a partner who can remember this in the midst of tension or conflict.

Their sensitive nature challenges them and they must learn to let go of their agendas for their loved ones and significant others. They do better when they step back and allow other people to stumble and learn from their mistakes, as their natural tendency is to intervene, rescue and protect. They are highly intuitive, psychic, and sensitive, and as a consequence, may deeply feel sorrow for the struggles of others and the burdens of the world.

Their higher intellectual understanding provides abundant wisdom and comfort that supports and nourishes them and they need to remember to tune in to this source, especially in times of turmoil. They may at times be moved to speak boldly and directly, and when they do so, can arouse a passionate response from others, for good or bad. They must ensure that they use this inner knowledge wisely to be of service to others and not to dominate them.

JULY 12 TO AUGUST 11
SOUL PROFILE: WILLFUL MEDIATOR

KEYWORDS

YOUTHFUL   ENERGETIC   ACTIVE   OUTGOING
INTENSE   WILFUL   LOVING   GENEROUS

The Willful Mediator is a natural leader who is charming, engaging and active in many different aspects of life. These souls feel what is right in a very deep way and don't necessarily respond to intellectual concepts or mental reasoning. They are motivated by spiritual will and when they know they are right, they act. They learn by experiencing life, rather than from organized courses of study.

Their natural energy arises spontaneously and can dissipate just as quickly. Though they are driven by love, they can be so determined to have things go their way that those around them may not recognize their deeper impulses. Like all Mediators, these souls want to reconcile all discord and create greater harmony in their lives and in the world. They are masters at bringing diverse energies into an integral and balanced expression. Their destiny involves conflict resolution, so they need to realize that they will always be surrounded by conflict in a variety of forms.

Willful Mediators are highly creative and often express themselves through writing, music or the performing arts. All Mediators are stars; they radiate exuberance and joy and appreciate being the center of attention. They maintain a childlike innocence, even when their expectations are extreme and their tempers flare. Trailblazers in many ways, they show humanity how to cooperate, expand and enlighten.

Though they can be intense in their expressions, these souls strive to balance and improve themselves and others by focusing the spiritual will into new and innovative endeavors. Their minds are illuminated from a higher plane, and they deftly strive to achieve maximum integration of this powerful force into the physical world. They are challenged to include other people in their heavenly schemes, rather than imposing their very strong will on them.

The greatest challenge for the Willful Mediator is to tame the ego and learn to share the spotlight with others. They need to find ways to ground their abundant energy, relax, and let go of their numerous expectations. When they do so, they find that the universe is working on their behalf and is always on their side. This soul's highest calling is to inspire, incite and inform.

Like the other Mediators, these souls are among the busiest in the world. They are typically surrounded by diaries, date books, calendars and schedules. They have a wide social circle and enjoy many different activities. They treasure all opportunities that allow their inner star to shine, and bring the praise and appreciation of those they seek to engage, educate and entertain. These magnificent and hardworking souls benefit from occasional retreats from the outer world to allow them to rekindle their light for their next adventure.

JULY 12 TO JULY 21
PERSONALITY PROFILE: 4 OF INTUITION
Passive Benevolence

KEYWORDS

| ORDERLY | NURTURING | PASSIVE | INTUITIVE | LOVING |
| REFLECTIVE | GENEROUS | PATIENT | | |

For all the fire of their souls, individuals in this profile can be quite passive at times. Their strong will often seems to exist only in the depths of the soul, and they may find themselves giving in to others even when it is not in their best interest. Their nature is primarily giving and nurturing, and they can quickly burn out if they do not learn to take time to recharge. When they tire of endlessly meeting the needs of others, they can be quite forceful in expressing their pent-up anger.

These individuals are highly intuitive, imaginative and often psychic. They enjoy the company of others, but also need time to themselves to reflect and regroup. They are primarily emotional, although their minds are also strong. They sometimes struggle to find sufficient energy to complete their goals and realize their dreams. They may be somewhat confused as to their direction in life, and gain greater clarity on this important subject by tuning into their souls.

Since they are highly receptive, they need to be careful what environments they enter as they will very likely take on the emotions and energies of others. This can result in mood swings, depression and withdrawal, which can be relieved whenever they remember to release all that they have picked up from their loved ones and friends.

They are quite visionary and intuitive, and this gift provides them with endless creative ideas. They can excel in music, art and theater, and also the mystical arts. Their challenge is to accomplish their souls' heartfelt mission while overcoming their natural tendency toward passivity. Their energy comes and goes, and is most accessible when they are independent of the day-to-day demands of their loved ones. Their natural instinct is to care for others, yet because they take in so much emotion from other people this can become a source of stress in their lives.

The more they can turn their attention to their creative drives, the more fulfilled and happy they will be. They do well when surrounded by creative collaborators and other supportive people who will give to them, rather than expect to receive. Their motivation fluctuates, and they often alternate between active involvement and passive disengagement. When they strike the right balance they are optimistic, happy and filled with joy.

These individuals are highly psychic with strong powers of recall. This potent mystical energy may appear as a desire to help others, alternating with retreats into quiet contemplation. The magnetic nature of their energy attracts attention from all in need. There is a tendency toward co-dependency and passivity, so they need to strengthen their will, and learn to maintain healthy boundaries. When they get in touch with their souls, they can master a higher level of compassion that perfectly balances their love with greater strength.

JULY 22 TO AUGUST 1
PERSONALITY PROFILE: 5 OF WILL
Mastering Challenge

KEYWORDS

PASSIONATE IMPULSIVE SELF-ASSURED WILLFUL
GENEROUS COMMANDING RESPONSIBLE BOLD

These individuals are driven by passionate desires. They do well when they can lead and inspire others. Life typically holds a variety of challenges for them, which they valiantly struggle to master. They are motivated by a sense of righteousness, which transcends any mental or emotional processes within them. This strength of will comes from the spiritual realm, and intermingles with an equally strong personal will.

This profile stimulates bold expressions in both words and action, which may sometimes result in quarrels and interpersonal conflicts. Their self-assured manner and insistence on perfection can create the impression of unkindness; however, deep inside they feel very responsible toward others and attempt to use their strong will to protect and defend their loved ones. They feel equally accountable in work settings and tend to give all they have to make things right in many situations.

Though they may be somewhat impatient, the individuals in this profile also have a great love for life and a natural affinity for all things spiritual. They do well as leaders, so long as they can manage their somewhat high expectations of others. Their frustrations stem from a sense of a higher order that is an inherent part of their world view. It is this higher realm that they are challenged to connect with and bring through to benefit others.

These individuals can be very generous, loving and enthusiastic. However, they need to feel appreciated, and when they do they are loyal and trustworthy in return. Their energy fluctuates and they often feel restricted internally in some way. Though they are more comfortable with a show of strength, they benefit from contact with their emotional side. This is not always easy for the Five of Will, but the rewards are many whenever they do get in touch with their feelings.

These individuals need to transmute their inner friction into spiritual confidence so that they can let their immense love shine through. When they realize that the discord, tension and conflict that surround them are actually lower expressions of a higher will to good, they gain mastery and grow in wisdom. As they learn to access the spiritual level of force that lies within them, they find that life offers them a unique and powerful opportunity to awaken to the divine.

AUGUST 2 TO AUGUST 11
PERSONALITY PROFILE: 6 OF WILL
Dramatically Triumphant

KEYWORDS

| HARMONIOUS | GRACEFUL | WILLFUL | ENTERTAINING |
| SUCCESSFUL | ENTHUSIASTIC | LEADER | SELF-FOCUSED |

These individuals thrive on relationships, social interactions and adventures of all kinds. Strong minded and willful, they can be successful in a wide variety of endeavors and occupations. Like their soul, the Willful Mediator, the Six is also a star, giving these individuals a natural tendency toward celebrity and fame. They genuinely appreciate beauty and are highly creative.

They present themselves to the world with great intensity, being driven by a spirit of joy, enthusiasm and love. They are eternally youthful and filled with innocence, even when their star-quality seems to demand that they be given the center stage and undivided attention. Though like all Mediator souls, they do not like conflict, they may not hesitate to throw a tantrum when they feel that no other strategy will help them get their way. This tendency mellows as they mature, and they have an opportunity to recognize that they are here, in part, to learn the lessons of cooperation. When they are able to moderate their personal needs, they enjoy being of service to others.

At times they can be willful and stubborn, and may engage in conflict to restore a sense of harmony and order. Though their self-focus is fierce, their personality is balanced overall, and they find many ways to share their generosity. When they learn to ground their exuberance, they make wonderful and inspirational leaders. However, it is important for these individuals to take time to rest and retreat from all of their worldly activities and involvements.

The Six of Will typically has financial success, and tends to establish a meaningful career. Their strength lies in the value they place on peace and harmony, and they will apply their powers toward these goals in every circumstance. They can be excellent mediators, reconciling conflicts and restoring harmony even if they have to resort to verbal force. They are challenged to use their leadership abilities to serve, rather than to dominate.

They need to discern if their desires are being generated from the level of spirit or ego and should learn to purify lesser desires and transmute them into expressions of benevolence and service. These individuals need to discover the difference between confident self-esteem and a need to receive admiration. As they transform their self-oriented, impulsive tendencies, they exude a commanding presence that assures their triumphant victory over all adversity.

AUGUST 12 TO SEPTEMBER 11
SOUL PROFILE: WORLDLY WARRIOR

KEYWORDS

SERIOUS   NOBLE   SENSUAL   ANALYTICAL   HARD-WORKING
RESERVED   PRACTICAL   INTELLIGENT

These old souls take on some of the greatest challenges in life. They are Warriors, adventurers and lovers of the earth. Like all of the Warrior soul types, these souls work with personality profiles that are energetically and numerologically distant from the soul. The personality tends to split away from the soul, and focus on its own agenda. This rift makes their challenge one of 'either-or', and they often find they must choose between the spiritual and the profane, heaven or hell.

The Worldly Warriors derive great satisfaction from work, and they often enjoy creating things with their hands. They are highly sensual and enjoy all aspects of earthly life. Internally they inhabit a dreamy world, understanding abstract concepts that go beyond language. They are intelligent and hold a great deal of wisdom, but they find it difficult to express their knowledge in words. They are somewhat reserved, a sign of their busy inner life. When they do engage with others they are delightful and charming, and they provide down-to-earth support to friends and loved ones alike.

These souls are passionate in their intimate relations, having a strong sexual nature that fuels their spiritual growth. They are quite intuitive and can use this gift to support the healing of their lover, partner or mate. Their attention to detail serves them well in love as it does when applied to their work. They need to watch their perfectionist tendencies and learn to find beauty in the chaotic emotions that commonly arise in love and also in family life.

Worldly Warriors love food, drink and all sensual pleasures, and their earthy nature may sometimes result in over-indulgence. They are typically well grounded in life and its realities, and need to watch for tendencies toward laziness and inertia. Their inherent interest in all aspects of nature can manifest through outdoor activities such as remote hiking and camping, the study of the healing properties of plants, gardening or any field related to the human body.

Warrior soul types come into life with a mission. They are noble souls invested in righteousness, and they will engage in defending the oppressed, persecuted and distressed in a variety of ways. Worldly Warriors bring relief and support to everyone whose lives they touch, simply by their gentle presence. These easy-going souls are adept at lightening up all circumstances with their sharp wit and lusty sense of humor. They are equally good at lending a sympathetic ear to those in need, and their sensitivity and loving ways endear them to everyone they meet.

AUGUST 12 TO AUGUST 22
PERSONALITY PROFILE: 7 OF WILL
Courageous Creativity

KEYWORDS

WILLFUL	COURAGEOUS	IMPULSIVE	CREATIVE
CONFIDENT	SENSUAL	EMOTIONAL	CHAOTIC

These powerful individuals are challenged to direct their abundant energy into heroic and creative actions. They are moved by an extraordinarily potent will. This gives them great power, for good or bad. When they are young, this energy tends to manifest in conflict, as they struggle to overcome a variety of obstacles. They are blessed with an inborn confidence that assures their ultimate victory over all challenges. They can bring a strong and determined approach to everything they undertake.

These individuals are motivated by emotion, passion and desire. They don't always think about the consequences before they act on their deeply felt impulses. They are highly creative, but need to learn to focus this energy so that it is not so scattered and unfocused. They may encounter some difficult circumstances in life that stand in stern opposition to their will. These circumstances teach them to persevere. When they do so, they find that they have sufficient energy and fearlessness to prevail and be victorious.

They feel a deep, spiritual sense of what is right, and will not hesitate to engage in arguments and strife if it seems necessary to help them bring their inner vision into outer reality. The purpose of this friction is to help them learn to focus on issues that are truly significant and not waste their valiant efforts on small and unimportant things. They are not naturally disciplined, and can benefit greatly from establishing a regular routine and more orderliness in their lives.

These individuals are very sensual and emotional. They feel their way through life, applying their inner senses to a great extent to help them attain their dreams. They are fairly ambitious and can do well in any field that allows their natural leadership abilities to come into play. Partly due to their acute sensitivity, they should guard against jealousy in relationships and an inclination toward envy and resentment in general. They need to remember to let go and trust that life will perfectly meet their needs.

These individuals can benefit greatly from spiritual study and practices. Whenever they can turn their intense energy inward, they are rewarded with the reassuring presence of their loving and noble soul. When they learn to transform the lower will into the higher, they begin to transcend conflicts, master their passions and attain their heart's desire. Their greatest gift is their creativity, which is nurtured and sustained by the natural world. Therefore, it is critical that they take time to immerse themselves in nature to strengthen and renew their spiritual connection.

AUGUST 23 TO SEPTEMBER 1
PERSONALITY PROFILE: 8 OF WORLD
Concentrating on Perfection

KEYWORDS

SENSITIVE   ANALYTICAL   PSYCHIC   HARD-WORKING
CRITICAL   HELPFUL   CAUTIOUS   CREATIVE

These individuals bring exacting practicality and attention to detail to everything they do. Their tremendous powers of attention ensure that no details are left out in even the most complicated tasks. In fact, they need to take care not to over-focus on small things at the expense of the big picture. They have high standards and are capable of true perfection; however, they need to learn that others may not be equally capable. Their precision assures that they will succeed in whatever they undertake.

These individuals grow in wisdom and gain materially through great effort and meticulous focus. They express their abundant creativity in a variety of ways, and are particularly adept when working with their hands. They are industrious and skillful, and are generally rewarded for all of their hard work. Though they can turn a critical eye toward any situation with success; they need to be sure they are not turning this power into merciless self-criticism, which they may be prone to do.

With a great interest in the natural world, these individuals enjoy the outdoors. Activities such as hiking, camping and gardening put them in touch with their souls. They are somewhat cautious, in work and in love. The advantages of their cautious nature include the great skill and carefulness they bring to their careers and their love lives. On the down side, this perfectionist quality can also result in pettiness and cunning.

Though they are hard workers, these individuals often find they receive only small gains for their efforts. They do better as they learn to let go of their desire for perfection, and apply their industriousness to the development of their inner, spiritual side. They can be highly intuitive, and are known as 'hidden mystics' due to their deep and rich inner life that links them to the spiritual world. They are highly sensitive and compassionate, and prefer to express these qualities in a devoted relationship. It may take them some time to feel comfortable and trusting in a relationship, but when they do so, they are among the most loving and considerate partners of all the profiles.

These individuals can be masters at detachment, due to the analytical gifts of their minds. They do well to apply this same objectivity to their loved ones and family members, where they usually have many karmic attachments in play. They spontaneously understand all types of symbolism, which can aid their spiritual awakening. Their great love of the earth can hasten the integration of their soul's energy into the personality, and they may even be drawn into mystical and occult studies when the time is right.

SEPTEMBER 2 TO SEPTEMBER 11
PERSONALITY PROFILE: 9 OF WORLD
Worldly Achievements

KEYWORDS

ORGANIZED PRACTICAL SUCCESSFUL WISE
SENSUOUS TENACIOUS CRITICAL DISCIPLINED

These individuals bring the energy of love and abundance into practical expression in the material world. They are careful planners who are able to focus on many details at once. Passionate about everything they do, they generally excel in any endeavor they undertake. They do well in money matters and use their assets wisely.

They are highly intuitive and spiritually motivated to bring greater awareness of the ageless wisdom into expression on earth. This mission may take a variety of forms; however, at some point in their lives, they may find themselves immersed in mystical, spiritual or religious studies. Naturally inclined toward the invisible realms, these individuals excel when they can share their spiritual gifts with others.

Individuals born within this profile are highly sensual, and oriented toward relationships that can satisfy their physical needs. They have a great love of nature and the earth, and are sometimes drawn toward the study of herbs, plants and natural healing. In all things, they seek harmony and peace, making them particularly adept as counselors, mediators and consultants.

Whatever they turn their detailed and precise minds toward will benefit from their analysis. They like their lives to be orderly and structured, which can prove challenging in relationships. They must guard against selfishness and the tendency to criticize others. Their focus on organization and attention to detail gives them great strength to accomplish their career goals, but may also alienate those close to them.

They are masters of perseverance, and almost always learn from their mistakes. However, they need to avoid turning their critical nature inward upon themselves. Learning to view themselves and others with detachment is the goal for these accomplished individuals.

These individuals will most likely be blessed with material abundance at some point in their life, whether through their own hard work and management skills, or through an inheritance or other good fortune. They are generally friendly, outgoing and good team players. However, they must learn to overcome a tendency toward obsession, as they may become overly involved in the details and lose track of the big picture.

As they learn to let go and share with others, they find greater expression of their deep soul impulse to be of service to everyone. They need to learn to value love above compliance with strict standards. When they overcome these potential obstacles in their path, they can be quite affectionate in expressing their love. These individuals are called to establish spiritual works on earth, and can attain great personal transcendence due to their natural wisdom.

SEPTEMBER 12 TO SEPTEMBER 22
SOUL PROFILE: INTELLECTUAL VISIONARY

KEYWORDS

LOGICAL   RATIONAL   SCIENTIFIC   INTUITIVE   COMMANDING
FORTHRIGHT   COMMUNICATIVE   GRACEFUL

These gifted souls bring great understanding and insight into the world, which reflects the highest ideals. They are both visionary and intellectual, receiving inspiration from the spiritual plane and then sharing it in a variety of ways. They are mature souls with a great deal of experience attained through previous incarnations. All of the Visionary soul types turn the wheel of the universe from one spirit type to the next. The Intellectual Visionary therefore oversees the last personality profile of the Willful consciousness, and the first two personas of the Intuitive consciousness.

They value knowledge, research and study, and not only know a great deal, but are very capable of communicating their knowledge to others. They are good with words, although not always patient, and have little tolerance for egotistical behavior, as they are more interested in bringing spirituality to the mundane world.

Like the other Visionary souls, these individuals are natural rulers and do best when they can lead, inspire and command others. This impulse may manifest as bossiness and a tendency to control and direct. They see so deeply into all circumstances that they instinctively know how to bring forth the greater truth that others may not perceive.

These souls are very compassionate and caring, yet they know intuitively when to stop giving and set limits out of love. Their commanding presence is almost always felt, even before they speak. It may take some time for them to understand their great power and the impact it can have on people. They are actually motivated by a heartfelt, nurturing, Goddess-centered energy, but need to realize that others may be threatened by their skill and dominance in verbal exchanges.

They love to study and often acquire libraries specific to their chosen field of knowledge. They are very intellectual and demand that all things be thoroughly tested before being accepted as true. These souls are often right, though they are not always graceful in expressing their point of view. They are gifted with words whether spoken or written, and are usually found teaching.

Keen observers, there is little that escapes the intent focus of these souls. They are able to detect deceptive or illogical thought processes, and appreciate open, orderly thought. They are especially sensitive to unrighteousness, and will take up any cause that appeals to their sense of fairness. Their impulses are based on a perfected truth that is difficult to realize on the physical plane. They are truthful and sometimes brutal communicators, for they will always tell you exactly what they think. For these souls, having a good idea is not good enough; it must have a purpose that will further the will to good.

SEPTEMBER 12 TO SEPTEMBER 22
PERSONALITY PROFILE: 10 OF WORLD
Reasonable Success

KEYWORDS

CLEVER   PROSPEROUS   LOGICAL   PRECISE   CREATIVE
IMPATIENT   INTUITIVE   GROUNDED

These individuals like all things of the earth and can do very well in material matters. They are excellent communicators, interested in bringing ideas to others in a very practical way. They could quite naturally be drawn to metaphysical studies, as they have a deep and profound connection to their souls.

They are attracted to commerce and are capable of acquiring great wealth, but as they are natural accumulators, they may just as easily accumulate possessions, followers or even weight. They are compelled to create something strong and enduring that will remain as their legacy when they depart the physical world. They may find that they accomplish their goals quite successfully, and then move on to bigger and better things.

These individuals will be interested in gaining property or money, but they will use their resources on behalf of others. Their mission involves advancing humanity, and they have the tenacity to succeed in whatever they undertake. Like all Tens, this profile has the greatest energy; however, they often feel that they have reached a plateau and no more energy is forthcoming.

In love they need to find a partner who supports their visionary mission and welcomes the abundant guidance and direction they tend to give to those they love. They require a partner who can keep up with their exuberant sexual energy. As parents they may overwhelm their children with suggestions, advice or demands. They need to learn to let go of the reins of power in relationships and let others act on their own. Even if mistakes are made, their loved ones will learn a great deal in the process.

These individuals are generally healthy and may be interested in work that involves healing others, especially natural forms of healing. They are reasonable and practical, but may be critical of others as they are able to perceive even the most subtle errors. Their tendency toward impatience needs to be overcome in order for them to advance spiritually. With all of the activities in their lives, they need to remember to escape into nature from time to time, as this will regenerate them and renew their dedication to their unique mission.

They do well when they can be creative, and will especially benefit from gardening, camping and all outdoor activities. They bring to the table the maximum understanding, energy and practicality, but need to learn to cooperate and let others have a turn at leading. They benefit from disciplines that encourage freedom from mental structures, such as dance and yoga. Such activities will aid them in discovering their creative abilities, and attaining the true wealth that comes from the divine.

Chapter 3

SEPTEMBER 23 TO DECEMBER 21

LIBRA, SCORPIO AND SAGITTARIUS

SPIRIT TYPE: INTUITIVE CONSCIOUSNESS

Transcendental Life

KEYWORDS

IMAGINATIVE   SENSUAL   VISIONARY   RECEPTIVE   CREATIVE
LOVING   ROMANTIC   EMOTIONAL

These elevated spirits have a very subtle presence. They are highly intuitive and visionary, and are motivated from the subconscious mind deep within. At the same time, they are often drawn to study and master complex systems of knowledge. They are creative mediators, and prefer harmony above discord in all circumstances. Among them are found natural mystics who perceive the spiritual realm and understand its language of numbers, archetypes and symbols. Through their souls and personalities they can ground these higher understandings on earth by sharing, teaching and inspiring others to learn and grow.

They are generous, giving and nurturing to their families, loved ones and anyone who comes under their care as students, apprentices or co-workers. They typically share their gifts through writing, art, music, teaching, counseling, the healing arts and education. However, they feel things deeply, and spend a lot of time considering their actions to ensure a perfect balance of emotion and mind. Their life lesson is that the mind can either help or hinder, and the heart is the only true guide to happiness on earth.

These individuals have a rich emotional life, and when it is not stifled by over-reliance on the intellectual mind, it can bring them deep satisfaction and enduring joy in their intimate relationships. They are often acutely sensitive to the moods and feelings of others, even when they are not verbally expressed. They value relationships and family, and will work hard to find the right mate and provide for their loved ones. They know intuitively that there is more to life than what appears on the surface, and they want to bring hidden things to light.

They are challenged to temper their over-generous nature and grow in self-esteem. Their soul grows when they learn to receive, realize and hold knowledge and wisdom in silence to benefit themselves, rather than sharing everything too freely with others as soon as it is received. They need to discern if and when helping others is really helpful, and learn to withdraw from those who are not willing or ready for change. When they turn their powers of perception inward, they receive great inspiration through their meditations and dreams.

They value privacy and are good at keeping secrets, but they usually don't appreciate it when others keep things from them. They are highly sensual and enjoy good food, wine and sex. They may have a tendency to soothe old wounds with these pleasures and need to beware of dependencies and addictions of all kinds. Their spiritual purpose involves the attainment of independence, autonomy and self-rulership in all things. They may have feelings of jealousy in intimate relationships that stem from subtle insecurities. In friendship, they are loyal and make every effort to keep or restore peace.

These spirits often see a vision of divine reality on earth, and they will seek to understand all technologies and traditions that may allow this perfection to manifest. They love to nurture and support others, and may be drawn to work that allows them to feed, nourish, teach, support or balance other people. They can be very passive due to their natural receptivity, and may be taken advantage of by others. When they strengthen their will they begin to gain greater mastery of their interpersonal interactions.

These spirits are capable of sensing things on behalf of others, but they need to develop the ability to remain quiet and allow people to manage their own struggles and challenges. Though they are generally happy, their great sensitivity may sometimes cause them to feel emotionally overwhelmed. In this case, they need to withdraw into themselves for a time, in order to rebalance and restore their energy.

They are typically good with words, especially when expressed in their journals, poetry or songs. Their verbal agility and the intensity they bring to arguments and conflicts is equally powerful. They value beauty, pleasure and romance in life, and their homes have a distinctive, aesthetic appeal. Gently charming and accommodating, they are almost always willing to help friends and family in need. Their interventions on behalf of others tend to be highly organized and practical, and they need to keep in mind the many benefits that can come from simply holding a hand.

These spirits are very insightful and can bring clarity and understanding to many diverse situations. They can be good consultants, and are able to see all sides fairly in dynamics between couples, partners or groups of people. When they pursue intellectual endeavors they excel at science, math, logic and systems. They may be drawn toward metaphysical studies such as astrology, numerology and spiritual psychology. They are natural leaders in any arena including the arts and humanities, human growth and development, natural or spiritual healing, technology and science. These spirits are here to reconnect to the balance deep within and must guard against extremes. Meditation, retreats and vacations are essential for their health and well-being in life.

These inspired spirits can establish far-reaching new works on earth. They carry within them a vision of a highly evolved and developed civilization that will create greater peace and understanding among all peoples and cultures. They will pursue philosophies – ancient, modern or cutting edge – that may one day allow this vision to come to life. They can see and reveal the deepest mysteries of life by remembering the divinity that lies within their own hearts.

SEPTEMBER 23 TO OCTOBER 12
SOUL PROFILE: INTELLECTUAL VISIONARY

KEYWORDS

LOGICAL   RATIONAL   SCIENTIFIC   INTUITIVE   COMMANDING
FORTHRIGHT   COMMUNICATIVE   GRACEFUL

These gifted souls bring great understanding and insight into the world, which reflects the highest ideals. They are both visionary and intellectual, receiving inspiration from the spiritual plane and then sharing it in a variety of ways. They are mature souls with a great deal of experience attained through previous incarnations. All of the Visionary soul types turn the wheel of the universe from one spirit type to the next. The Intellectual Visionary therefore oversees the last personality profile of the Willful consciousness, and the first two personas of the Intuitive consciousness.

They value knowledge, research and study, and not only know a great deal, but are very capable of communicating their knowledge to others. They are good with words, although not always patient, and have little tolerance for egotistical behavior, as they are more interested in bringing spirituality to the mundane world.

Like the other Visionary souls, these individuals are natural rulers and do best when they can lead, inspire and command others. This impulse may manifest as bossiness and a tendency to control and direct. They see so deeply into all circumstances that they instinctively know how to bring forth the greater truth that others may not perceive.

These souls are very compassionate and caring, yet they know intuitively when to stop giving and set limits out of love. Their commanding presence is almost always felt, even before they speak. It may take some time for them to understand their great power and the impact it can have on people. They are actually motivated by a heartfelt, nurturing, Goddess-centered energy, but need to realize that others may be threatened by their skill and dominance in verbal exchanges.

They love to study and often acquire libraries specific to their chosen field of knowledge. They are very intellectual and demand that all things be thoroughly tested before being accepted as true. These souls are often right, though they are not always graceful in expressing their point of view. They are gifted with words whether spoken or written, and are usually found teaching.

Keen observers, there is little that escapes the intent focus of these souls. They are able to detect deceptive or illogical thought processes, and appreciate open, orderly thought. They are especially sensitive to unrighteousness, and will take up any cause that appeals to their sense of fairness. Their impulses are based on a perfected truth that is difficult to realize on the physical plane. They are truthful and sometimes brutal communicators, for they will always tell you exactly what they think. For these souls, having a good idea is not good enough; it must have a purpose that will further the will to good.

SEPTEMBER 23 TO OCTOBER 2
PERSONALITY PROFILE: 2 OF INTELLECT
Peaceful Balance

KEYWORDS

INTELLIGENT   DIPLOMATIC   VISIONARY   SENSITIVE
COOPERATIVE   INTUITIVE   INDECISIVE

These sweet-natured individuals are gifted with a close affinity to their souls. They are primarily interested in balance and harmony, and will go out of their way to keep the peace in all circumstances. They are highly intelligent and equally interested in science and the humanities. Partnership is very important to these individuals, and they will go to great lengths in relationships to be sure that all is fair.

They are great diplomats and mediators, and are especially gifted at supporting cooperation. However, at the same time they are very strong individuals, and won't hesitate to speak their mind when necessary. They are rational and logical, although they may sometimes sacrifice these gifts in order to avoid facing their emotional dependencies. They have a keen sense of balance and typically seek to find the middle ground in all circumstances.

Personal, romantic relationships are very important to these individuals. They do better when they have a loving and supportive partner. However, they may also linger too long in relationships that are not supportive, out of their overblown sense of fairness. In such cases these individuals struggle to learn to stand up for themselves and not sacrifice their own needs as a way of avoiding conflict. They have a tendency to repeat offenses if they are once forgiven for them.

In this personality profile, these individuals receive a great deal of inspiration from their exalted and visionary souls. They seek to express higher ideals through artistic means, in their work and their lives. They are extremely sensitive, and it is this acute sensitivity that leads to their desire for perfect balance. When such perfection cannot be established, they may feel inadequate, as if they have failed. They need to learn that the perfect harmony they sense in their souls may only rarely be realized on the physical plane.

Though they have a love of study and typically attain academic degrees, their intellectual capabilities are actually derived from their intuitive spirit. They understand the divine reasoning that makes all science possible, and they work diligently to manifest that higher vision on earth. They may sometimes withdraw into their inner world, which is filled with beautiful and ethereal ideas. However, they can be equally adept at expressing some of these transcendental concepts through writing, speaking and teaching others.

As they learn their own worth and develop their unique wisdom through the cultivation of their own self-esteem, they gain in strength. Their mission is their own spiritual empowerment, which can position them to bring greater tranquility and unity into the world. These individuals need to remember to take time out from all of their abundant mental activity, which can result in tension and stress. As they discover the power and serenity that comes from regular immersion in silence, they attain the balance within that allows them to master all that lies without.

OCTOBER 3 TO OCTOBER 12
PERSONALITY PROFILE: 3 OF INTELLECT
Intelligent Compassion

KEYWORDS

COMPASSIONATE INTELLECTUAL REFINED MOODY
SELF-FOCUSED INSIGHTFUL COMMANDING SELFISH

These sensitive individuals have a fierce compassion for others. Their highly sympathetic nature can create a sense of loss and sorrow, as they are acutely aware of all human suffering. As with all Threes, these folk must guard against a certain instability that can manifest as moodiness and attempts to control others and their surroundings. They have strong minds and are generally intelligent. This personality profile has the same numerology as the soul, which gives these individuals a very high vision to fulfill.

Their natural tendency is to be commanding; although their intention is for the good, they want their ideas to prevail. If they do not receive respect for their ideas, they may feel defensive and become willing to fight for their ideals to manifest. They value logic and reason, yet it must be in service to the highest compassion. They are very refined and do not care for gross expressions.

In personal relationships or working partnerships, they prefer to be in charge. Their natural tendency is to focus on themselves, which comes from the desire to see their higher ideals expressed in the world. They are family oriented, and do well in relationships that allow them to take the lead. Their great sensitivity makes them naturally empathic toward others, and they must be careful not to take on other people's emotional turmoil.

These individuals do best when they can put their powerful minds to work. They are not too physically inclined, but prefer projects that involve writing, creating or expressing intellectual concepts in a way that benefits others. They are changeable, energetic and enigmatic. These qualities often lead others around them to wonder who they really are.

These individuals have undertaken this life for the purpose of completing all of their karma. Due to this, it is highly possible that events in their current life will be re-creations of those from past lives. These karmic dynamics will be reflected in their relationships with friends, enemies and intimate partners. They are blessed by a balanced understanding that helps them remain centered as they witness the clearing away of old patterns, and release themselves from past attachments. They need to remember to stop trying to control outcomes and simply move on.

They benefit greatly from forming a relationship with the right partner, which helps them transcend the miseries of a troubled world and attain greater wisdom. They are motivated to seek peace with others, but when they are unable to achieve this, they may feel very unhappy. They can become compassionate healers and effective humanitarians as they let go of their past, surrender to the wisdom of the soul and become liberated from the illusions of separation.

OCTOBER 13 TO NOVEMBER 12
SOUL PROFILE: INTUITIVE MEDIATOR

KEYWORDS

VISIONARY   PASSIONATE   MYSTICAL   COOPERATIVE
INTUITIVE   CREATIVE   STRONG-WILLED   COMPASSIONATE

These youthful and energetic individuals are highly visionary. They are good at balancing a variety of opposing energies and making them into a harmonious whole. They are very active, having a rich social life in addition to mastering many work-related tasks. Their mind and emotions are generally balanced, and they can attain an intellectual understanding of their mystical visions and experiences.

The energy of these souls can be quite powerful, and they could be considered spiritual cyclones. They can tap into the universal unconscious and draw upon its dynamic energies. They are clever and wise, and often find themselves in a position of leadership on behalf of others. Their inner nature is very intense; however, this is seldom revealed by their calm exteriors.

They prefer to avoid conflict at all costs, and generally try to mediate in any discordant situation. They are motivated toward peace and will do whatever it takes to restore serenity in the midst of chaos. Equilibrium is very important to these individuals in every aspect of their lives. Due to these special gifts, they may often find themselves in environments that are far from peaceful. This is particularly true of their childhood home, where they first learn and master their gifts of mediation.

These souls typically find themselves in situations where their unique abilities as a peacekeeper are most needed. This allows them to strengthen their natural qualities. As they get older, they understand their powers better and tend toward more harmonious and cooperative relationships. Nevertheless, they can always be relied upon to provide gentle guidance and advice whenever it is needed

These souls are very gifted and creative. They love to care for others in a variety of ways. They are particularly drawn toward sharing mystical wisdom, expressive and healing arts, and food for the body and the soul. Their piercing insights give them a profound understanding of what lies beneath virtually any dynamic they find themselves within. They need to learn how and when to apply their powerful will and intervene to restore fairness.

There is far more to these gifted souls than what they may reveal. They carry ancient wisdom deep within them, and subtly use it to benefit everyone. Yet they seldom reveal the sacred knowledge they hold. They have great respect for secrecy, whether it involves the protection of esoteric secrets, or the private lives of their friends. These souls are loyal, loving and kind, and they offer their abundant blessings to everyone they meet.

OCTOBER 13 TO OCTOBER 22
PERSONALITY PROFILE: 4 OF INTELLECT
Defending Peace

KEYWORDS

| ORDERLY | COMMANDING | COMPASSIONATE | CHARMING |
| SPIRITUAL | PASSIONATE | RIGHTEOUS | COOPERATIVE |

These gregarious individuals bring a wealth of gifts to the world. They willingly enter situations of conflict on a mission to restore peace. Their approach to life is orderly and contained. They have a strong intellect, which is nicely balanced with the emotional and intuitive influence they receive from their souls. Unless they are overwhelmed by the pain of human suffering, they maintain a fine equilibrium within themselves.

These individuals have great love and compassion, and their kind nature endears them to everyone. They can be unusually charming, and they enjoy social and community gatherings. Others often find them charismatic, and they are typically very attractive. They are as serious in their work as they are light-hearted in love. Due to the strength of their minds, they must guard against suppression of their emotions.

They are generally loving and forgiving; however, they can also be fierce when their passion is aroused. This fierceness typically arises wherever they perceive unrighteousness or encounter an unfair situation. They have a great sensitivity toward the underdog and will do all they can to defend those in need. Aside from their warrior-like tendencies, they generally serve as mediators, focused on restoring the peace.

When they are in harmonious surroundings, they are entertaining and beneficent, sharing their gentle humor and graciousness with everyone they meet. They are highly spiritual individuals and capable of great mercy, but they may have a tendency to be overly giving, and need to learn to shift from caretaking into a higher, more detached compassion. They are generally relaxed and serene, and insist on the expedient resolution of all conflict.

These individuals particularly love relationships and are dedicated their partner and family. They are inspired by a higher vision for humanity, and others feel confident and secure in their presence. Their philosophical and empathic nature is particularly well-suited for all work involving service to others. They excel in situations that demand excellent and fair mediation, as they can encourage compromise and resolution with their keen insights.

These individuals generally experience good things in life, and are adequately taken care of in terms of their material needs. They are hard workers who do best when they have a structured environment and can apply their unique supervisory abilities. As peacekeepers, they have a very positive gift to share, but must realize that clearly defined limits can also prevent hostilities from ever beginning. They may need to strengthen their will in order to master the lessons set up by their soul.

The peace these individuals seek is really a divine peace, which seldom looks like the human version. This peace is truthful in a non-emotional way, looking dispassionately at all sides of any issue. It is the peace that surpasses understanding, because it perfectly balances mercy and justice, giving and limiting, love and power. This is the focus and goal for these individuals as they strive to balance will and love, and find the true peace that lies within.

OCTOBER 23 TO NOVEMBER 1
PERSONALITY PROFILE: 5 OF INTUITION
Transcending Discontentment

KEYWORDS

DREAMY   SENSITIVE   MOODY   EMOTIONAL   EMPATHIC
SELFISH   INTUITIVE   SENSUAL

These individuals often carry a deep and profound sadness inside that has its origin in previous lives. They are generally languid, as they tend to enjoy relaxation more than effort, and they can be stubborn at times. They experience life on the emotional level, preferring their mystical understanding to intellectual pursuits. They are passionate and can be forceful in their expressions.

They have powerful psychic abilities and tend to feel their way through life, responding to an inner prompting that others may not understand. They tend to resist structure and discipline, and will withdraw rather than submit to an outside, organizing influence. They are generally passive, reserving their more passionate expressions for intimate encounters that allow them to feed their highly sensual nature.

A core challenge is to balance their sensitivity and engage with others in a more cooperative way. They have a tendency toward selfishness, which shows their intense inward focus. Though they are generally docile, they can secretly harbor resentments that build up inside and then explode in fits of rage and jealousy. When they do speak out against slights or mistreatment, they may have little control over their words and express themselves sharply. They can also be quite dramatic as they attempt to get others to meet the needs they feel so acutely.

These individuals may be prone toward melancholy and have a hard time letting go of things, people and environments that they enjoy. This letting go is the key theme for their experience in this life. They feel any loss intensely, and may try to hang onto things that are no longer useful to them. These disappointments reflect an emotional turmoil that is generated from the level of their souls.

Often these individuals have experienced a tragic death or loss of a loved one in a previous incarnation. These past life memories may be very deeply buried in the soul; however, if they can be accessed through spiritual counseling, much healing may be gained. When they recover from these inner wounds, they may be able to benefit others with their unique psychic abilities.

They are attractive and magnetic, and their challenge is to develop greater self-discipline and temper their relentless desires. They do best when they find a supportive relationship that fulfills their highly sexual needs and nurtures their sensual nature. They must keep in mind that their relationships offer an opportunity to overcome self-focus and transmute unhappiness into love.

Because they are highly creative and sensitive, they can excel in work that makes use of their artistic abilities and natural empathy.

Art or music therapy, dance, theater or professional counseling may be suitable careers. They can also do well as psychic readers, spiritual healers or clairvoyant mediums should they choose to develop these skills. The most important consideration is that they clear their own emotional turmoil through direct, expressive means before they attempt to help others do the same. Their highest calling is to complete their lingering karma, learn to laugh and be free.

NOVEMBER 2 TO NOVEMBER 12
PERSONALITY PROFILE: 6 OF INTUITION
Pleasurable Success

KEYWORDS

MYSTICAL   SENSUAL   WISE   LOVING   EFFICIENT
AMBITIOUS   RESOURCEFUL   STUBBORN

These loving and generous individuals are among the most ambitious and successful of all profiles. They exist in close proximity and harmony to their souls, and consequently have access to a deep pool of mystical wisdom. They enjoy all of the pleasures of life, and are especially happy when they can share their love and wisdom with others.

They are especially masterful at reconciling conflicts, and often find themselves in leadership positions. They prefer their environment to be harmonious and will do whatever it takes to maintain balance and peace. This is due in part to their highly sensitive nature, but also provides an outlet for their unique mediating skills.

These individuals tend to achieve success wherever they focus their attention. They are ambitious by nature and strive to advance in their careers. Their many talents are rewarded and they often find that they have many responsibilities to manage. Their inherent resourcefulness ensures their continued success. Though they may meet challenges along the way, there is little that they cannot master or attain.

These innate qualities endear them to others, and they are thrilled when they find their true partner in life. In relationships they are loyal and loving, and appreciate sharing their sensual gifts and skills in intimacy. They can be quite emotional and may struggle with feelings of jealousy. Though they are generally patient and kind, when angered, the result can be sharp criticism and sarcasm.

Often these individuals find themselves engaged in professions or enterprises that involve food or feeding others. This provides an outlet for the abundant feelings of love and nurturance that they have come into the world to express. They are also highly artistic, and typically find that the culinary arts fulfill their desire to please others with their impressive knowledge and abilities.

Their strong desire for pleasure brings with it the determination to see it fulfilled. When they are driven by this force, they can be quite stubborn and unyielding in the quest to have their way. The key to mastering this energy is for them to learn to focus their desires toward the spiritual plane. When they do so, they can become powerful transmitters and revealers of the mysteries in service to the divine.

NOVEMBER 13 TO DECEMBER 22
SOUL PROFILE: WILLFUL WARRIOR

KEYWORDS

INTENSE   NOBLE   WILLFUL   GENEROUS   CONFIDENT
SELF-FOCUSED   ARROGANT   IMPULSIVE

These ancient souls take on a variety of missions in life that are motivated by an unspoken understanding of the universal abstract wisdom. They are typically very strong-willed, powerful and independent. They take their mission in life seriously, yet they struggle at times due to the energetic and numerological distance between them and their personalities.

They are usually happy when they can serve as motivators, innovators and initiators of others and create new works on earth. Their endless energy supports them in getting started on their quests; however, they may not always have sufficient energy to follow through and complete the tasks they undertake. They alternate between impulsive, sudden actions and reactions, and withdrawal, retreat and repose.

Like all Warrior soul types, these souls face the greatest challenges in life. These difficulties occur in order for them to gain greater experience and soul-growth. They reach for great heights and often find themselves confronted with several all-or-nothing situations. They must choose between the high road of spirit and the low road of personal gratification.

These souls are projective by nature and do not easily receive from others. They are expressive, but may at times feel misunderstood as they struggle to share the deep wisdom they hold. They may be impatient, and can be quite intense as they defend what they believe to be right. They can be so relentlessly independent that they may become very disconnected from others.

These souls operate beyond language and structure, and are primarily motivated by sheer force of will. Their energy is abundant and they respond intensely in the moment, not always considering the impact of their words on others. They carry the fire of life and want to awaken that spirit within everyone they meet. They want to establish their will and have it prevail. As they mature, they learn to leave bossiness behind and focus on leading others to the light.

These souls enjoy leading and teaching others, and don't do as well in dynamics where they are expected to listen to people whom they do not perceive to have knowledge equal to their own. However, they have a tendency toward haughtiness and arrogance and need to be sure that their opinions or beliefs are actually superior before they dismiss the views of others. Often just the presence of these powerful souls can make others feel threatened, and it may take some time for them to understand why this occurs. The power they carry is very great and always provokes strong reactions, whether it appears as devoted adoration or fearful rejection.

Depending on their personality profile, their extraordinary will can result in good success in all aspects of life. The challenges they undertake take time to master and they are engaged in this pursuit over the course of their entire incarnation. As they learn how to use the immense force they hold, they inspire others to find their passion, express their creativity, restore their health and align with spiritual truths. When they accept their calling to bring the divine will to bear upon the earthly plane, and temper their fiery gifts, these exhilarating souls can activate and bring forth celestial powers and direct them to bring greater good to humanity and the earth.

NOVEMBER 13 TO NOVEMBER 22
PERSONALITY PROFILE: 7 OF INTUITION
Sensual Indulgence

KEYWORDS

IMAGINATIVE   PASSIVE   SENSUAL   INTUITIVE   PASSIONATE
CREATIVE   SECRETIVE   INTROSPECTIVE

These individuals are extraordinarily sensual, and interested in all things related to physical love. They are highly intuitive and could easily live in their own rich internal world, rather than engage in worldly existence. Their lives often consist of a series of tests, offering a choice between a powerful spiritual life and wanton self-indulgence.

Their capacity for desire, which is immense, is derived from a great unconscious source, and their many visions, dreams and inner imagery are profound. However, they have a tendency to take these perceptions at face value, and they can become a source of confusion. The task of these individuals is to learn to discern what is real and what is illusionary. Their psychic abilities are truly a gift from their spirit; however, they can feel overwhelmed by the abundant imagery that passes before their inner eyes.

Though they are drawn to relationships, which are an important outlet for their overwhelming sensual impulses, they can find it difficult to express their deeper feelings to a partner. Their energy is primarily emotional, and it is difficult for them to put their experiences into words. They need to guard against indulging in fantasies, which may only increase their intense sexuality, and lead them into further daydreams and delusions.

Over time they find that healing, teaching and inspiring others can help them connect them more concretely to the outer world. When they can transmute their erotic impulses into spiritual energy, they begin to unfold the key to their soul's mission in life. They often find they must choose between the lower and higher expressions of this powerful force. Their path is earthy, and their visions have their root in mystical and shamanic past lives.

These individuals are attractive, and offer many creative gifts to the world. Because they live primarily in their inner world, they may find it difficult to form lasting alliances. They may be tempted by and attracted to intoxicants of all sorts. They need to guard against obsessive tendencies, compulsive behaviors and addictions in relation to substances or food.

They are generally passive, but can be quite outspoken when they are provoked. They find themselves distracted due to their abundance of desires, and may have difficulty sustaining action in any particular field. As they become aware of their higher purpose in life, they will need to establish a stronger self-discipline to help them reach their goals. Though they may struggle with it, they do better when they undertake structured courses of study.

These gentle individuals quickly realize that, for them, there is no middle ground. In order to meet the demands of their destiny, they must turn their amorous tendencies into spiritual force. Spiritual practices that can aid them in this transmutation may include meditation, yoga and esoteric study. When these individuals attain their self-mastery, the benefits are tremendous, and their limitless wisdom can be creatively expressed through art, music, and healing work.

NOVEMBER 23 TO DECEMBER 2
PERSONALITY PROFILE: 8 OF WILL
Instantaneous Inspiration

KEYWORDS

INTELLIGENT   PHILOSOPHICAL   WILLFUL   NARCISSISTIC
IMPULSIVE   IMPATIENT   ANALYTICAL

These freedom-loving individuals are inspired by lofty philosophical ideals. They tend to accumulate knowledge in a variety of subjects, often without completely mastering any one discipline. Their love is of study itself, and they find that what they learn simply validates what they already know. They enjoy sharing their abundant knowledge with others.

They like to be informed, and may be drawn toward researching, teaching and organizing information. They are family-oriented and enjoy groups, gatherings and classes of all kinds. They are readers, writers and thinkers who love ideas and concepts. Because they are highly intellectual, their greatest challenge is on the emotional level.

These individuals are willful and impulsive, and typically prefer to get their own way. Their energy is somewhat scattered, and they can be unfocused as their intense concentration wanes and moves them onward to new topics. This is due to erratic, inner energy that causes them to become easily bored. They fluctuate between action and rest, and sometimes feel frustrated that their energy is not sustained. At the same time, their rather self-centered approach to life may encourage them to justify their down-time and indulge in periods of laziness.

It is important that they take time to access their passion, but to do this they must let go of ingrained belief systems that they commonly apply toward the repression of their feelings. They can develop an egocentric nature as they prefer to avoid sensitive emotions and consequently imagine they are above it all. They need to watch out for a tendency toward arrogance as they become highly invested in their opinions and beliefs, even when they are wrong. They do better when they get out into nature, undertake physical activity and practice silence. It is important for them to allow their mind to rest from its quest for information.

These individuals are self-confident, and often act boldly and courageously. They are willing to defend their beliefs and any philosophies that they feel they have mastered. Their minds are quick and they can be formidable opponents in argument and debate. It is better for them to direct these traits to assist and educate others, rather than to allow them to devolve into self-righteousness or pompous conceit.

Overall, their minds are constructive and they like to apply themselves to positive endeavors. They may be somewhat isolated, but are friendly when social situations come along. They enjoy organizing activities, if they can keep their attention focused on the task. They like to be free from the control of others and prefer to be their own masters. In love they are passionate and intense, but they will not settle for less than their ideal match. This is a wise way for them to proceed because they need to have a partner who can help keep their energy focused on the spiritual quest.

They are not particularly good at holding their tongues in the presence of ignorance and do not always get along with other strong-willed individuals as they will battle for their right to be right. With such strong minds, they are often in a state of mental tension. When they learn to better access their soul energy, they find that they can think less and tap into tremendous motivation. This is because their soul energy exists beneath the level of the mind and operates as deeply felt impulses that arise from within. They do best when they make time to express their creativity through art, poetry or music.

An ethereal wisdom exists naturally within them, which they can only grasp by attaining communication with the soul. When they seek this victory above all else, they come into their spiritual gifts. Their primary mission is to let go of the mind and surrender the lower will to divine authority. By embracing humility and giving up their tightly held beliefs, they gain liberation from past karma and contribute to advancing the consciousness of humankind.

DECEMBER 3 TO DECEMBER 12
PERSONALITY PROFILE: 9 OF WILL
Determined Inspiration

KEYWORDS

HEALTHY   SENSUAL   INDEPENDENT   INTUITIVE
SUCCESSFUL   SELFISH   CONTENTIOUS   BLUNT

These enthusiastic individuals bring a sense of purpose into everything they do. Like all of the personality profiles within the Willful Warrior soul type, they have a mission to accomplish in life. They are generally healthy and full of energy. Their abundant optimism comes from their deep intuitive connection to the bright spirit within.

They are typically outgoing and generous toward others. Their strong personal will sustains them in attaining their goals. These individuals can be successful in a variety of careers. They have a sense of what is right and fair, and bring that to bear wherever it is needed. They can easily move between outward activity and inward contemplation.

They may often find themselves in a position of providing support to others. They can be good listeners, but will quickly speak out if they see a solution to a problem. They are hard workers, but do better when they can work independently. Their natural leadership ability often finds them directing, managing and inspiring.

They benefit from physical activity, which helps them manage their abundant energy. They are not so much intellectual as they are intuitive, and motivated by deep impulses from their souls. Their expressions are direct, and they need to learn to temper their words as they may appear blunt or tactless.

These individuals have tremendous endurance, and the ability to follow through when they are passionate about their objectives. Though they are generally positive, they can have periods of moodiness that signal a need to go within for a time. They feel compassion for all of life, and tend to focus on how they can contribute to the improvement of humanity.

Their inner vision provides inspiration that stimulates their strong willed nature, and feeds their souls. They see deeply into all circumstances, and want to make things right. They may be quite forceful in these attempts, and need to learn patience and tolerance. They are very sensitive and often have an interest in metaphysical subjects.

Their primary calling is to understand the true nature of existence, and to use that knowledge to be of service to others. They are confident and outspoken, and may find themselves drawn to public service, or guiding and teaching. It is important for them to align with and follow their inner guidance in all aspects of their life.

These individuals carry a highly spiritual energy that illuminates a profound purpose in life. They are kind and generous in love, but must guard against dominance toward their partners. They are highly sensual and very loyal when they find the right partner. Relationships are important to them as they serve to provide a safe resting place from their active outer lives.

The intensely spiritual nature of this profile will guide these individuals in all they do. This unseen source of their power is capable of bringing success and victory even in situations that may appear hopeless. Their tenacity and commitment can serve them well; though they need to learn that their will does not have to prevail at all costs. When they turn toward spiritual life, they can awaken a powerful current of energy within their bodies and direct it to initiate greater consciousness on earth.

DECEMBER 13 TO DECEMBER 21
SOUL PROFILE: WORLDLY VISIONARY

KEYWORDS

**CHARMING   KIND   INTUITIVE   INTELLIGENT   CREATIVE
COMPASSIONATE   TENACIOUS   SERIOUS**

These attractive, magnetic and earthy souls bring tremendous spiritual gifts to the world. They are naturally humble and carry great love in their hearts. They receive and share great spiritual insights, and have an enlightened approach to life. Their spontaneity and charm endear them to all they meet. All of the Visionary soul types turn the wheel of the universe from one spirit type to the next. The Worldly Visionary therefore oversees the last personality profile of the Intuitive consciousness, and the first two personas of the Intellectual consciousness.

These souls are highly creative, and find satisfaction in art, music, dance, theater, writing and all acts of passionate expression. They are experienced souls, having had many incarnations. Due to this they bring great spiritual understanding into every circumstance. Because of this innate wisdom, they are often drawn toward the service of others in healing, counseling or humanitarian works.

They may feel misunderstood by others, because of the rich nature of their inner life, but they are capable of understanding just about anyone. They are interested in establishing material works, which allow an outlet for their abundant creative energy and permit them to leave an enduring legacy.

They are often quite serious, which reflects their sensitivity to the people, circumstances and events that surround them. They are deep thinkers, highly intelligent and analytical. Yet they must be careful not to keep their mental gifts in sterile isolation from their compassionate hearts. They seek to bring refinement and greater realization of divine wisdom to the human experience.

They are often physically attractive, an outer manifestation of the beauty of these souls. They have a deep affinity with nature and are lovers of the earth. They have an instinct for natural healing, and prefer holistic systems that encompass the spiritual aspect of the human as well as the physical. At the same time, they appreciate the science behind these arts.

These souls bring great spiritual energy into the physical body. They are sensual, not only in their intimate relationships, but in their entire experience of earthly life. They are highly psychic and intuitively pick up on the subtle thoughts and reactions of others. Due to this, they may be cautious in divulging the deeper feelings they hold inside.

These individuals are generally practical, orderly and organized. They are gifted with words, and talented at helping others whether through educating or inspiring them. They can be quite sociable, and are equally adept at leading and being a good team player. They especially enjoy gatherings that focus on the exchange of ideas, innovative concepts and creative activities.

These gentle souls bring truth, wisdom and their own unique insight to everyone they meet. They are loving and lovable, and instinctively know when to share their abundant knowledge and when to listen in their quiet and supportive way. They are family oriented, and conscious of the good of the whole. They share their special gifts with their loved ones and the human family, leaving everyone better off for having met them.

DECEMBER 13 TO DECEMBER 21
PERSONALITY PROFILE: 10 OF WILL
Material Dominion

KEYWORDS

| WILLFUL | ENERGETIC | GENEROUS | OVERBEARING |
| RESPONSIBLE | INTUITIVE | INDEPENDENT | AUTHORITATIVE |

These determined individuals bring an abundance of energy into every aspect of their lives. They are highly independent and motivated to succeed. They are driven by a powerful spiritual force and determined to accomplish their mission in the world. They are particularly talented at material things.

They are driven by their unique mission, which may take many forms. They are quite clever, and good at overcoming all obstacles. Their will is so strong that they may alienate others in their quest to accomplish their goals, and their greatest challenge is learning to balance the overbearing force that makes them natural leaders, but also creates self-centered desires.

When they feel they are being obstructed or limited in any way, their response can be volatile and explosive. They need to establish command of their tremendous power and direct it for the good. They have an ability to detach and view things from a higher perspective, which gives them dominion in virtually any arena. They seek out and often attain positions of great responsibility.

When they find appropriate outlets for their forthright nature, they can become quite generous and inspirational. They are very intuitive and could use this gift to benefit others. They are capable leaders and do best when they have the greatest freedom to express their own will. Though they prefer to lead, it is important for them to learn to cooperate with others. This is a critical lesson that has its roots in past life experiences where they may have been overly cruel or self-interested.

They come into the world to establish a unique and enduring legacy, and are quite capable at managing all aspects of business, finance and real estate. Their independent nature and personal quest often precludes long-term relationships. They do better with partners who are equally enthusiastic about their mission, and willing to support their goals and ideals. They need to work to transcend their overbearing tendencies and learn to share control.

These individuals tend to be quite successful, as they are capable of overcoming any opposition. They are generally well-spoken and well-informed in their areas of expertise. They can benefit from meditation and introspection, which provides opportunities to direct their energy inward. As they expand their minds and awaken their souls, they may be empowered to detach from material things and gain the spiritual treasures of the kingdom within.

Chapter 4

DECEMBER 22 TO MARCH 20

CAPRICORN, AQUARIUS AND PISCES

SPIRIT TYPE: INTELLECTUAL CONSCIOUSNESS

Transmitting Ideals

KEYWORDS

| INTELLIGENT | COMMUNICATIVE | RECEPTIVE | COMMANDING |
| INSIGHTFUL | REASONABLE | IMAGINATIVE | COMPASSIONATE |

These gifted spirits maintain a delicate balance between receiving inspiration and sharing it with others. They naturally resonate with higher ideals, and these elevated understandings contain the essence of life itself. They are imaginative as well as intellectual. The power they carry is very great, and it comes to them through their minds. They define, give order to and put words upon subtle and abstract wisdom.

Though their soul and personality profiles vary greatly, their spiritual mission remains the same. It has to do with the accumulation, contemplation and transmission of knowledge and information. They receive their inspiration from the spiritual plane, but tend to verify it by immersion in academic studies, research and scholastic endeavors.

They are generally balanced between active and passive expressions of love. As they teach and share with others, they activate within them the quest for a more conscious life. They are insightful and intuitive, and have an inherent sense of when to give and when to hold back. They can be powerful channels who receive transmissions from the eternal source and project them out to the world in practical applications.

They project a strong, reassuring and healing presence to others and are able to make complex knowledge accessible through art, music, speaking and writing. Wise spirits, they are strong communicators and may express themselves sharply and intensely. They will find that their powerful presence may feel threatening to some, and they need to remember to avoid those who react to them in this way.

Their logical, rational nature depends upon an intellectual force, which does not occur spontaneously or naturally, but must be continuously called into being. Due to this, they can feel mental weariness and suffer from stress. Because their minds are so active, they may experience emotional, physical and mental tension. It is important for them to know that their spiritual power can be renewed by focusing on the breath in silence for several minutes.

When they consciously let go of ideas, concepts and words and breathe deeply, they are restored and nourished.

Their home, clothing and material possessions show their graceful and artistic nature. They are sensitive to environments and to other people, and they do best when their surroundings are beautiful and serene. Their protective nature can evoke fierce reactions, and provide an outlet for some rather stern and serious expressions. They prefer to follow their own authority and take command of their life or career direction. This makes them ideal team leaders, rather than members of a team.

They are often creative, poetic and precise. Some of them enjoy a unique ability that causes their ideas to appear in physical reality as art, books or theater. As they materialize their ideals, they are attempting to bring heaven down to earth. These are lofty spirits who prefer to follow their own path. Though they are better at working alone, they can work with others, but will need to at least be in charge of their own area of responsibility and in a position of relative independence.

The intellectual inspirations that these spirits bring forth can stimulate new scientific understandings, create innovative systems and technologies and renew spiritual ideals. They are here to help humanity wake up and evolve, but they need to develop diplomacy and avoid domineering or controlling attitudes.

The highest use of their inherent spiritual energy is in leadership, particularly intellectual leadership. What they have to share comes from a pure source of knowledge, and relies upon will and imagination for its expression. As much as they love knowledge, they are here to learn to go beyond it, and they benefit from activities that allow them to go more deeply into emotions, passion and intuition.

These spirits are capable of very great love; however, it is an elevated love, and in that sense it is a more pure force. The compassion they feel serves the spirit when it becomes the compassion of a Buddha, but to achieve this, they must avoid a tendency to coddle and care for others in a codependent way. They are able to see the reasonableness of love, but need to develop discrimination.

Their energy is all encompassing, and they give 100% of their attention to whatever they choose to contemplate, learn or teach. They are adventurous, penetrating and forthright. They want to look into things, see what is really there and make decisions based on what they surmise. They seldom miss any details and are always able to keep the big picture in mind.

These spirits naturally prefer harmony, but will not avoid conflict when they find an opportunity to establish a higher good. They can be great mediators as they have an ability to see all sides of any situation. It is important for them to find physical activities that they enjoy, and exercise on a regular basis. Being in nature helps relieves their overly active minds, giving them a chance to breathe easy, rest and connect with the earth before beginning their next adventurous quest.

DECEMBER 22 TO JANUARY 9
SOUL PROFILE: WORLDLY VISIONARY

KEYWORDS

CHARMING   KIND   INTUITIVE   INTELLIGENT   CREATIVE
COMPASSIONATE   TENACIOUS   SERIOUS

These attractive, magnetic and earthy souls bring tremendous spiritual gifts to the world. They are naturally humble and carry great love in their hearts. They receive and share great spiritual insights, and have an enlightened approach to life. Their spontaneity and charm endear them to all they meet. All of the Visionary soul types turn the wheel of the universe from one spirit type to the next. The Worldly Visionary therefore oversees the last personality profile of the Intellectual consciousness, and the first two personas of the Worldly consciousness.

These souls are highly creative, and find satisfaction in art, music, dance, theater, writing and all acts of passionate expression. They are experienced souls, having had many incarnations. Due to this they bring great spiritual understanding into every circumstance. Because of this innate wisdom, they are often drawn toward the service of others in healing, counseling or humanitarian works.

They may feel misunderstood by others, because of the rich nature of their inner life, but they are capable of understanding just about anyone. They are interested in establishing material works, which allow an outlet for their abundant creative energy and permit them to leave an enduring legacy.

They are often quite serious, which reflects their sensitivity to the people, circumstances and events that surround them. They are deep thinkers, highly intelligent and analytical. Yet they must be careful not to keep their mental gifts in sterile isolation from their compassionate hearts. They seek to bring refinement and greater realization of divine wisdom to the human experience.

They are often physically attractive, an outer manifestation of the beauty of these souls. They have a deep affinity with nature and are lovers of the earth. They have an instinct for natural healing, and prefer holistic systems that encompass the spiritual aspect of the human as well as the physical. At the same time, they appreciate the science behind these arts.

These souls bring great spiritual energy into the physical body. They are sensual, not only in their intimate relationships, but in their entire experience of earthly life. They are highly psychic and intuitively pick up on the subtle thoughts and reactions of others. Due to this, they may be cautious in divulging the deeper feelings they hold inside.

These individuals are generally practical, orderly and organized. They are gifted with words, and talented at helping others whether through educating or inspiring them. They can be quite sociable, and are equally adept at leading and being a good team player. They especially enjoy gatherings that focus on the exchange of ideas, innovative concepts and creative activities.

These gentle souls bring truth, wisdom and their own unique insight to everyone they meet. They are loving and lovable, and instinctively know when to share their abundant knowledge and when to listen in their quiet and supportive way. They are family oriented, and conscious of the good of the whole. They share their special gifts with their loved ones and the human family, leaving everyone better off for having met them.

DECEMBER 22 TO DECEMBER 30
PERSONALITY PROFILE: 2 OF WORLD
Unity through Change

KEYWORDS

BALANCED   HARMONIOUS   PARTNERSHIPS   ADAPTABLE
LOVING   EARTHY   PASSIONATE   INTUITIVE

These insightful individuals are highly adaptable, earthy and passionate about everything to do with the physical realm. They possess an extraordinary intelligence; however, their knowledge comes from a deep, inner realm that makes it difficult to share with others. Their proximity to the soul's numerology indicates that they are conscious of their roles as vehicles for spiritual love and wisdom.

These individuals typically experience great change in their lives. This is not a negative manifestation, but a part of their creative nature. They can go with the flow, as long as they guard against a slight tendency toward stubbornness, and are often aware of a definite sense of timing and rhythm that subtly directs their lives. They enjoy all kinds of work, especially where they can make use of their excellent communication skills, but they may change careers several times.

They are sensitive, psychic and naturally harmonious, and will seek to restore balance in all chaotic situations. They prefer to always have a partner, as relationships are very important to them. However, they are here to learn to bring balance to their own needs and guard against a tendency to over-focus on caring for others. At the same time, they benefit from relationships, and when they don't have a partner, they are generally unhappy. Their relationships are often highly spiritual, since they desire the perfect union of body and soul.

The somewhat aloof nature that others may perceive in these individuals is often a sign they have retreated into the rich, silent recesses of their souls. This internal process aids them to access unique and innovative ideas that they can bring to fruition in the material world. They are drawn toward nature, the outdoors and all things of the earth, which replenishes their energy and inspires their spirits.

These individuals are primarily practical, creative, organized and helpful. Their life circumstances may shift between losses and gains in money, assets, and property. Their emotions and moods can cycle between happiness and sadness, determination and apathy, and outspokenness and withdrawal. As they learn to master the fluctuations between extremes, they can find a center point of stillness that allows them to surrender and adjust easily to all circumstances.

The key to their ability to synthesize diverse forces is their higher awareness of the inherently spiritual nature of the physical plane. These individuals tend to have strong self-control, yet are able to remain flexible and responsive to changing situations. This can aid them greatly in financial, career and family matters. They should not hide their spiritual wisdom, but learn to consciously remain open to the rhythm of abundance at the heart of the manifest universe.

DECEMBER 31 TO JANUARY 9
PERSONALITY PROFILE: 3 OF WORLD
Enlightening Humanity

KEYWORDS

| PRACTICAL | PRODUCTIVE | CREATIVE | COMMANDING |
| INDEPENDENT | VISIONARY | SUCCESSFUL | DISCIPLINED |

These highly enterprising individuals can be found assisting business development, introducing innovative art and design, launching original enterprises and achieving financial success. They are inspired to manifest ideals that come from a higher source. They have a natural understanding of life, and powerful visionary abilities. Generally fearless, their high ideals may lead them to attempt things that others would consider impossible. However, their challenge is to temper their ambitious nature to ensure that their goals will fully manifest before they move on to their next inspiration.

Sweet-natured and loving, these individuals are family-oriented and seek lasting relationships and friendships. Their practical approach to life serves them well at home and in their careers. They are passionate and sensual, and typically prefer intimate partners who understand the spiritual nature of sexual union. They may have periods of moodiness and feel somewhat emotionally unstable from time to time. This is due in part to their great sensitivity, which may lead them to take protective measures such as withdrawal, when what they really want and need is love. Their fear of losing love can sometimes inhibit them in relationships.

They can overcome any fears of emotional pain by recognizing and remaining connected to the abundant spiritual love that lies deep within them.

These creative individuals may become bored if they are not busy building on or sharing their many talents. They prefer a disciplined and constructive environment, and do well when given the greatest responsibility. Though they are independent, they are also good team players. They often end up working for themselves in order to have the freedom to realize their visions in the material world. Their soul's mission is to establish unusual and enduring expressions of the higher mind on earth.

Their self-reliance, spiritual insights and prophetic visions can result in business success and contribute great things to the enlightenment of humanity. They have a commanding presence, can be clever in commercial transactions, and will generally benefit in all money matters. Their interests are varied and may include architecture, fashion, music, writing, technology, graphic design, education and science. They seldom have only one focus in their lives and work, tending instead to express themselves in several key ways.

They have an affinity for all things of the natural world. Though their souls are elevated, they are also earthy. Time spent in the outdoors can restore their energy and nurture their souls. Their visions for cultural transformation may involve the creation of new ways for people to live in harmony with the earth and nature. They may take an interest in healing with herbs, food and natural substances. They may also find that their bodies respond better to natural healing methods than to synthetic drugs.

These talented individuals strive to establish and maintain order and rulership in virtually every setting, especially in their home environment where they are gentle but firm parents, watching out for the good of all. They are both intelligent and wise, and value knowledge as much as intuition. Yet they need to learn to embrace their place in the world as solitary visionaries who may not be understood by others. It is important for them to remember that they are not here to be understood, but to understand and bring aid to others. As they overcome feelings of isolation and loneliness, they are assured of constant companionship on the inner planes.

JANUARY 10 TO FEBRUARY 8
SOUL PROFILE: INTELLECTUAL MEDIATOR

KEYWORDS

THOUGHTFUL   INTELLIGENT   CAREFUL   BALANCED
CAUTIOUS   SOCIAL   WELL-SPOKEN   YOUTHFUL

These active souls bring gifts of superior organization into every realm of life. They are highly intelligent and interested in acquiring great amounts of knowledge. They prefer peace and will apply their talents in skilled mediation to resolve all conflicts. They are energetic and youthful, and are typically involved in many different activities that keep their social calendars full. They are full of ideas and can apply their creative gifts to manifest their higher vision.

Intellectual activity is their primary hallmark; however, they synthesize the mind with the heart, and look for ways to share their love of knowledge with others. They are skilled communicators and teachers, and are typically found surrounded by books and information technology. Their natural strength of mind may cause tension and stress reactions. The breath is their secret power and when they take time out to breathe and relax, they let go of their endless flow of thoughts and their energy is restored.

It helps them greatly to consciously connect with their bodies and the earth. Physical exercise is very important in helping them maintain their health and release mental stress and tension. Nature is the complementary force to their abundant intellect. They may find themselves involved in caring for the well-being of people, animals and the earth. These souls do well when they spend time outdoors on foot, by bike or in water.

They prefer to avoid disagreements and strife; but the soul's mission is to balance and harmonize all kinds of oppositional dynamics. Consequently, they typically find themselves in situations of imbalance endeavoring to negotiate amicable settlements. They are not only able to reconcile issues between people on the physical plane; they are also skilled at creating awareness of the inherent unity of the physical and spiritual worlds. Simply by their presence, they perform an unseen service to their loved ones. They moderate and empower deeper soul connections for any family members or significant others in need.

As reconcilers between spirit and matter, they are comfortable in the invisible, ethereal world. This makes it somewhat difficult for them to feel at home in the mundane world. They are here to assist and lead others; but they need to receive attention from others as well. Like all of the Mediator soul types, they are stars who radiate knowledge, joy and peace to others. Their inner light shines brightly, and they can become real celebrities in their chosen fields.

These souls compassionately see life's deeper truths in an observant and detached way. This aids them in giving good advice to others. Because they see things clearly, they can usually find superior ways to attain success and sustain cooperation. They are equally receptive and projective – receiving inspiration from the inner planes and then giving it out to the world; however, they should strive to hold their knowledge in silence at times, so they can receive its benefit. They need to develop the ability to quietly listen, withholding their lightning quick insights so that others may struggle and grow.

They may have an interest in metaphysical studies, wisdom traditions and spiritual philosophies. These systems clarify and validate many of their unique perceptions of life. They have a special connection to angels, if they choose to focus on them. These souls convey a sense of pure innocence, and desire to see perfection in a largely imperfect world. When they remember the true reality that lies beyond the veils of the manifest world, they come alive in spirit and radiate God's own grace.

JANUARY 10 TO JANUARY 19
PERSONALITY PROFILE: 4 OF WORLD
Earthly Power

KEYWORDS

PATIENT GIVING ORDERLY PRACTICAL MYSTICAL
PASSIVE EMOTIONAL STUBBORN

These individuals are generally very organized and grounded. They value order, and strive to better the world through practical initiatives. Primarily emotional, receptive and passive, they tend to be overly generous and often lack a strong will. They have capable minds and prefer to apply their wisdom toward material works. Though they are competent workers, they are sometimes merely good starters who may struggle to complete tasks and projects.

They can be susceptible to manipulation and being taken advantage of by others. Because they are so giving, they often have trouble setting and keeping healthy boundaries. In family and personal relationships, they tend to be overly concerned about the opinions of their loved ones, often sacrificing their own needs and self-worth in the process. They are here to become independent, activate their inner strength and embrace a self-directed life.

These individuals can be natural and gentle leaders who may do better in their careers when they can work for themselves. When they find their passion, which allows them to express their unique creativity, they can be tremendously successful. They are detailed planners who work hard to manifest results. Their efficient nature serves them well; however, they are prone to worry, which can sometimes set them up for failure. Overall, they are patient and diligent even if they may be overly cautious at times.

They are earthy and benefit from spending time in nature. Natural nurturers, they make excellent parents so long as they remember that appropriate limits are a part of love too. They may at times feel suspicious of others, and have a tendency toward intolerance in their youth. Over time, they learn that other people are not always as quick-minded and sharp as they are, and they need to temper their somewhat critical nature.

They can attain great material and financial success, but do best when they find ways to use their assets in service to others. They have a highly mystical nature, which may be somewhat hidden, and can be powerful mystics if they learn how to awaken their supernatural powers. Their mission is to balance the material world with an infusion of spiritual force.

These individuals can be excellent mediators and diplomats, but may be prone toward too much compassion when firmness might be better advised. Though they tend more toward weakness than power, they can learn to strengthen the will by working consciously with their physical bodies. Regular exercise, getting into nature, and undertaking spiritual study, yoga and meditation can help them find a better balance within. Their highest calling is to connect to their spiritual source, and drawing upon that, serve as a conscious mediator between the spiritual and material planes.

JANUARY 20 TO JANUARY 29
PERSONALITY PROFILE: 5 OF INTELLECT
Willful Mind

KEYWORDS

INTELLECTUAL   IDEALISTIC   DETERMINED   WILLFUL
SELFISH   CHANGEABLE   UNPREDICTABLE   ALOOF

These individuals are very intellectual and inspired by higher ideals. They are drawn toward study, investigation and knowledge. They are likely to have some conflict and tension with others throughout their lives. In all their endeavors, they may experience swift, unexpected endings, which they are able to manage due to their ability to approach life without sentimental attachments.

They can sometimes manifest significant psychological repression, because their strong mind will tend to suppress uncomfortable emotional reactions. They often feel a constant strain, which may lead to worrying about potential defeats and difficulties. This can result in feelings of anxiety, which are a sign that they need to refocus and let go of unwarranted concerns. They are typically amiable, though they may seem rather aloof. Their cool, calm demeanor is evidence of their unusual detachment from emotional involvement.

These individuals can be short tempered, and may be prone to verbally assail others when provoked. They can also be manipulative, clever and evasive; though they are often able to find constructive outlets for these tendencies, such as career advancement. Some individuals in this profile may slander others, as they are prone to engage in idle gossip. Their efforts to avoid powerful emotions that may be lingering deep inside of them may arise from a lack of sufficient affection in their childhood homes.

In relationships, they are not possessive and are very independent. They need to seek a partner who will be a friend, and help them to let go of the pain of the past. They are here to learn to express the warmth and understanding that they desire from others. While generally cautious when choosing a mate, they are loyal partners and dedicated parents when they find the right person.

These individuals can be found surrounded by calendars, journals, notebooks, papers, documents and computer files. These outward objects reflect their intent focus on developing and using their superior organizational and mental powers. They are adept at handling a multitude of tasks and problems, and are well equipped to bring them to a successful resolution.

They bring a youthful, exuberant energy to everything they do, and are excellent mediators. Consequently, they often find themselves working with all types of conflict, and dealing with people or situations that are out of balance. Their mission is to bring harmony and peace through intelligent analysis. These individuals are equally capable of receiving knowledge and giving detailed information to others. They may find themselves playing the role of peacekeeper in their families and other relationships.

These powerful individuals are strong willed, and will sometimes attempt to dominate others. They can command any argument in a dispassionate way, which gives them an advantage in the intellectual arena. They are challenged to balance this intellectual nature by coming into greater awareness of their sensitive, emotional and spiritual levels of being.

Their minds are filled with high ideals, but their karmic lessons are about balancing strength with mercy and love, and learning to soften their words and express compassion. They are very good at seeing the multi-faceted nature of any situation and finding a way to resolve things fairly, but they frequently operate from the mind alone, in separation from the heart. They need to realize that the emotional level of life has equal value to the logic of the mind. What looks reasonable to the mind is not always reasonable to the heart.

JANUARY 30 TO FEBRUARY 8
PERSONALITY PROFILE: 6 OF INTELLECT
A Scientific Approach

KEYWORDS

INTELLECTUAL   PATIENT   HARD-WORKING   OPEN-MINDED
LOVING   CONVENTIONAL   HARMONIOUS

Quick-minded and highly intellectual, these individuals see the value of harmonious relationships in all areas of life. Because their minds are so active, they must learn how to take time out from thinking and relax. They are wise and practical, independent and robust. They can work with others, but do better when their natural leadership abilities are allowed to shine. They have a strong and clear connection to their souls, and this allows them to be aware of higher realities and ideals.

These individuals have an exuberant nature, and are typically found managing many projects, activities and social engagements. Their natural mediating abilities cause them to become involved in conflicts and unbalanced circumstances where they can support a restoration of peace and balance. Though their minds are strong, they are heart-centered and compassionate, able to bring reason and compassion into perfect expression

They are often drawn to the study of science, especially when it helps them to be of service to others. They may be found in the fields of medicine, mathematics, chemistry, biology and natural healing, and are often drawn to things that combine heart and mind such as theology, religion and metaphysical systems. They like to study, read and attain knowledge that they can share in helpful ways. They are also quite creative and can find pleasure in dance, music and the arts.

They exude a great deal of energy on behalf of other people, thinking and reflecting deeply about them and their needs. They are especially attentive to their mate, children and loved ones, ensuring that all of their needs are met. They are sensuous lovers and practical parents. They can be spiritual healers and have a unique gift for chanting sacred sounds and words, should they choose to pursue such a discipline. They are like a radiating star, giving out light and love. In return, they need to have acknowledgement and attention from others.

They like to have a philosophy that can guide them through life. They are inspired by higher ideals and feel frustrated if they cannot make their visions manifest in the outer world. They can transform spiritual impulses into physical action, and strive to bring a perfected precision into life. They can gain relief from mental stress and tension by getting involved in non-intellectual pursuits such as shamanic journeys, trance-dancing and drumming. They need activities that will allow them to go beyond the mind and experience divine chaos. Once they have had some time out from the mind, these individuals will enthusiastically return to their abundant mental pursuits.

These hard-working individuals accomplish their goals with a combination of their penetrating insight and straight-forward approach. They are open-minded and able to express their unique understanding with great clarity. Disciplined, original and intelligent, they share with the world their higher vision of the interconnected nature of all things.

FEBRUARY 9 TO MARCH 10
SOUL PROFILE: INTUITIVE WARRIOR

KEYWORDS

SENSITIVE INTUITIVE PSYCHIC SENSUAL GENEROUS
GRACEFUL MOODY SELFISH

These old souls are among the most experienced, and they take on demanding challenges in their lives that are defined according to their personality types. They use these obstacles to grow in wisdom and love. They are completing karma and mastering soul tendencies that they have brought forward from many previous lives. As they meet these tests and trials, they strengthen the connection between the spiritual and material worlds.

They are highly receptive to the intellectual consciousness, which is their spiritual type. They intuitively perceive higher ideals by way of their profound inner vision. The intuitive consciousness gifts these souls with a remarkably creative imagination that manifests in ideas, premonitions and dreams. They apply their strength of will to ensure that their deep inspirations will have a definite effect in the world. They have acute sensitivity to unfairness, and willingly take steps to restore righteousness at all costs, allowing them opportunities to refine their Warrior nature and hone their battle skills.

Like all of the Warrior soul types, these individuals have a natural affinity for higher knowledge. Their lofty ideals and comprehension of complex concepts and systems draws them inward. They are somewhat reserved, very private and not easily understood by others. It is hard for them to give words to the abstract wisdom that they intuitively grasp. They are responsive to energy and vibrations, and gain greater insight into people and circumstances with this expanded awareness.

Due to their depth of perception, they tend to follow their own inner impulses and are seldom swayed by others. They may seem a little distant from the world and they often have the experience of being misunderstood. They cannot easily explain their interior state to others as their gifts lie beyond all words. Nevertheless, people enjoy the company of these noble souls because they are good listeners and are almost always pleasant to be around.

They are naturally sensual and graceful, preferring beauty and harmony in their personal surroundings and homes. They may be poetic in their expressions, and are primarily gentle and loving.

Their usual serenity can be disturbed when they are provoked by arguments or disputes, but it would take a serious battle to activate intense reactions because they prefer to remain calm. They get along well with others and tend to keep unfavorable opinions to themselves, which brings them success in cooperative endeavors.

Being Warriors, these observant individuals have a special mission to accomplish in life. The form this will take depends upon the qualities and nature of their personality type. In general, they are skilled at teaching, studying, helping, healing, defending and nurturing. In social settings, they enjoy the company of long-time friends and colleagues. They enjoy a variety of leisure activities, and especially anything involving water. Because they are emotionally oriented, they can be easily affected by surrounding energies and people. When they find themselves becoming moody, they must remember to guard against unconsciously taking on emotional projections from other people.

Their soul may feel a little disconnected from their personality, and very remote from the concerns of daily life, so they may find themselves brooding over how to make sense of the outer world. This can generate inner tension, and they do much better when they take time out and relax. They often pick up random, discordant impressions from others, and need to spend plenty of quiet time within their internal world. At the same time, they need to balance their tendency to withdraw protectively, and learn to share their private thoughts with their loved ones and significant others. The challenge is that when they do so, they may still not feel completely understood.

Relationships are a compelling necessity for many of these souls. They want to be in the right relationship, and may seek this ideal throughout their lives. It might be some years before they find the right match, because they need a mate who is truly capable of understanding their mysterious soul. They are loving and generous, and a good friend to anyone in need, but they do better with a partner who can match their sensual, physical intensity. They may have tendencies toward selfishness and need to learn to share with others.

The Intuitive Warrior dwells within the celestial plane of consciousness, yet works with personalities enmeshed in the material world. Finding the right balance between spiritual impulses, sensual cravings and acute psychic awareness is a core task for these souls in life. Their mission involves learning to master the powers of these divergent worlds, and synthesizing the contradictory energies that flow between personality and soul. When they master this alchemy, their spiritual mission begins – to awaken others to divine ideals and hidden, invisible worlds.

FEBRUARY 9 TO FEBRUARY 18
PERSONALITY PROFILE: 7 OF INTELLECT
Ambitious Initiatives

KEYWORDS

CREATIVE   EMOTIONAL   SENSUAL   INTELLIGENT   INTUITIVE
PASSIONATE   UNSTABLE   STRONG-WILLED

These innovative individuals are in service to others, working to bring a vision of a better world to life. Possessing a strong intellect and a highly developed intuition, this combination of contradictory energies may make them feel unbalanced at times. It can take some time for them to become established in life because their interests are variable and subject to change. They relate strongly to their inner feelings, but also subject those feelings to intense mental analysis.

Their passionate nature is obvious, as whenever they feel deeply about something, they may impulsively act upon it. It helps them to have an organized system or philosophy with which they can align themselves. Although they are capable of sharing in-depth information with others, they may do so in a scattered manner. They are naturally artistic and creative, and it is good for them to find ways to express themselves that make the most of these gifts.

These individuals are challenged to discern when and where to share their advanced insights. What seems self-evident to them is not often apparent to others, due to the elevated nature of their soul. They tend more toward acting upon what feels right than any organized, structured approach; however, they benefit when they can develop better boundaries and learn to work within practical limits. They need to learn to bring out their rational, logical side and not rely solely on inner awareness.

They are exceptionally strong willed, and this supports them in defining and accomplishing their mission in life. Though they may be somewhat rebellious in their youth, as they mature they acquire the ability to let go of deep-seated desires for control and seek greater cooperation. They are highly intuitive and may have psychic abilities. If they rely on these tendencies alone, they may go astray because their unique mission includes developing logic and reasoning skills. These counter-balancing qualities can help them discern between what is real and what is illusion.

In love, they are generous and nurturing. They prefer to be surrounded by familiar loved ones and friends. However, life may require them to travel quite a bit, which helps them learn to let go. They can be quite outspoken because of their definite opinions and their tendency to argue to win. Conflict is likely to arise at these times, as they passionately advocate for their beliefs. They have to guard against being overly defensive and learn to live and let live.

They gain rewards from spiritual study and guidance that can help them get in touch with the soul. Without establishing an enduring link to this elevated energy, they become overly mental and their words can be tactless and explosive. They are somewhat ego-identified, which represents a primary challenge for the soul. Their highest calling is to be humanitarians and contribute to the evolution of society and civilization.

Although they intuit the deeper levels of life, these individuals may have some difficulty understanding other people. When they can reconcile their own internal divisions, they become better able to manage their behavior toward others. It is important for them to find the right partner in life who can provide consistency and stability. They usually need to spend some time mastering their highly sensual nature before committing to a monogamous relationship. Unless they experience the full range of sexual expression with a variety of partners, they may be tempted to fulfill this need even if they are involved in an exclusive, devoted relationship.

These individuals need to remember to take time to go deep within themselves. Meditation, yoga and physical exercise can bring them greater stability. Their greatest lesson is to develop concentration. Their abundant ideas seldom run dry, but they don't always have sufficient focus to bring them into worldly expression. They need to realize the power and presence that naturally flows from them, even when they do not speak. Others may sometimes feel threatened by them and they do well to avoid these personality types. Those who are at ease in the presence of these intense and vital individuals can benefit greatly from the many gifts and inspiration that they are here to freely give.

FEBRUARY 19 TO FEBRUARY 28
PERSONALITY PROFILE: 8 OF INTUITION
Healing Beliefs

KEYWORDS

INTELLIGENT   INTUITIVE   FRIENDLY   NURTURING
GRACEFUL   PASSIVE   ALOOF   CALM

These gentle individuals have the unique gift of intuitive intelligence. They feel things deeply and instinctively discern the vibrations that lie beneath the surface of words and actions. They may feel pulled in two different directions – the spiritual realm and the material world. Their challenge in life is to integrate spirit and matter in order to heal old patterns and wounds. As they mature they become better equipped to meet this demand. Spiritual study and conscious living are important factors in their mastery of the diverse forces they perceive within.

Due to their strong intellect and loving hearts, they are ideally suited to be teachers, parents and guides. They can also be highly creative, expressing themselves through art, music or poetry. Their lives are often very busy, and yet in the midst of it all, they can begin to feel weary and are pulled to withdraw. Their energy is not always consistently sustained and they can feel quite depleted at times. This signals the healing crisis that often plays a key role in their life. In one form or another, these individuals will return to the theme of healing themselves many times.

Due to their innate receptivity, they have access to a deep reservoir of wisdom within. This wisdom is beyond words and experienced primarily as intuitive knowledge; however, they have the ability to convert this ethereal knowledge into words. Due to this talent, they make very good advisors for their loved ones and friends. They have a subtle presence that endears them to others, even when their personal energy is running low.

They need to be careful about which philosophies they choose, because wrong beliefs are often the cause of their emotional and physical ills. They typically enjoy study and readily take on concepts that help them develop a cohesive world view, but they need to guard against involvement in value systems that rely on the provocation of guilt, shame and fear. They are too sensitive to bear the impact of harsh religious ideas, and should look instead toward traditions that affirm the goodness of humankind.

In love, they are nurturing and supportive. They make good parents, provided they continue to heal the internal distress that may linger from past difficulties in life. They are charming and sociable, and tend to develop long-term, close friendships. Though their energy drops at times, they typically persist to attain their dreams, and work steadily when they are refreshed. Their determined nature allows them to slowly but surely manifest what they desire, step-by-step, progressively moving forward.

These individuals generally have an affinity for the cycles and rhythms of life. They are adept at weaving connections between others, bringing them together in social groups and activities of all kinds. They can hold cherished beliefs that are hard to let go because they have served them well at some point in life. Therefore, they need to realize the impressionable nature of their personal energy field, remind themselves to detach from ideas and break free from the mind in order to touch the soul.

These individuals are challenged to experience the non-intellectual side of life. They are very orderly and organized and tend to avoid chaos and disorder. In this regard, they may also repress natural bodily energies and desires. It is healing for them to learn to free their sexual energy and enjoy the sensual aspect of life. Whatever aids them to open the body to greater feeling can stimulate their healing as well. For some, this may be shamanic arts, hands-on healing or exposure to some of the sexual healing principles of Tantra.

MARCH 1 TO MARCH 10
PERSONALITY PROFILE: 9 OF INTUITION
Wishes Fulfilled

KEYWORDS

SENSUOUS   SUCCESSFUL   BENEVOLENT   PEACEFUL
MOODY   SELFISH   INDEPENDENT   PSYCHIC

These lovable individuals intuitively understand the deeper mysteries of life. They are capable of sensing intentions and predicting outcomes due to their natural psychic abilities. They are often aware of the invisible worlds, receiving contact from deceased loved ones and disincarnate spiritual guides. Due to their ability to detect the energy and motives that underlie spoken words, they can be successful in whatever they undertake. They are often secretive about their clairvoyant abilities, reflecting their overall tendency toward privacy. Although they enjoy spending time with friends, they are also likely to withdraw from people completely at times. During these solitary moments they enjoy relaxing at home, in nature and especially on a beach.

These individuals are graceful and calm, bringing an atmosphere of serenity to every encounter. They are good listeners, and due to their cautious and quiet nature, they appear to be supportive and understanding. Even when they are reacting internally with disgust or displeasure at what is being said, no one will suspect their true feelings due to their reserve. Their private life is sacred to them and they may go to great lengths to protect their solitude and personal relationships.

Love is very important for these individuals, and they will typically persist in relationships even if a significant other is not really good for them. They take their time with commitments in love because they value their independence. Though they are generous and loving, they are paradoxically somewhat selfish as well. They work hard for their success and prefer to keep any material gains for themselves. This can lead to disruption in relationships, and it highlights one of their greatest challenges in life, which is to learn to share and cooperate rather than cling to possessions for the sake of greater control.

In work they are diligent and persistent, and typically engaged in endeavors that allow them to be of service to others. They are primarily non-judgmental and are able to work with a wide variety of people. They do better when they work for themselves as they don't always get along in groups. They have fairly high standards, which they are easily able to meet; however, they may not have sufficient patience to cooperate with others who are less capable. Though they are generally quiet, they have tremendous passion within them. They can hold their own in any disputes due to a sharp and detailed mind.

These individuals are extremely sensitive to environments and other people. They take on and reflect discordant energies, negative emotions and incidental stress. As they mature they become better at protecting their personal space. This is one reason they place high value on their private time. Recreational activities and regular exercise are critical to help them maintain their balance and deeply unwind. However, their strong drive to work soon propels them back into the material world.

They are extraordinarily physical in a highly sensual way. They need to have the freedom to explore this inherent power without religious or social constraints. Their sensuality connects them to their soul and they are motivated to seek a loving partner whose energy matches theirs. When they find the right partner in life, they are loyal, devoted and happy. Their intimate life is active and robust, and intensifies their passion, but they are challenged to elevate this abundant force into spiritual directions as well. They need to expand their expressions of love, and they would do well with a partner who has equal sensitivity to the unseen worlds and devotion to a spiritual path.

Gregarious, charming and kind, these individuals are often physically attractive and a pleasure to be around. They are dedicated friends who maintain social relationships for long periods of time. Their metaphysical interests create opportunities for exploration and growth, and their mission in life is to awaken others to the subtle worlds. When they master their psychic abilities, they can serve as excellent guides. They may be drawn toward teaching, healing or advocating for others. When they master their passions and learn to share, they can succeed in the most important goal in their lives – to be a noble warrior sensing a better way for humanity to establish a higher life.

MARCH 11 TO MARCH 20
SOUL PROFILE: WILLFUL VISIONARY

KEYWORDS

STRONG-WILLED   COMMANDING   CHARMING   IMPULSIVE
HOT-TEMPERED   CHEERFUL   LOVING   INTUITIVE

The Willful Visionary is a soul with great power. They are often quite determined, but may express this in a passive way. They are motivated by a non-intellectual impulse that gives them an internal feeling of what is best, right and good. All of the Visionary soul types turn the wheel of the universe from one spirit type to the next. The Willful Visionary therefore oversees the last personality profile of the Intellectual consciousness, and the first two personas of the Worldly consciousness.

They have to ensure that their dominant nature does not result in an obsessive need for control. When they feel righteous, they can easily get into difficulty with others. Their motives are innocent however, as they really do want to bring about the highest good. They need to realize that friends and family members have to make their own mistakes and learn from them, and they are not likely to respond favorably to bossiness.

Their strength of will also endows them with great enthusiasm and determination to attain success in life. They are more sensitive and sympathetic than they may at times appear. They receive inspiration from the intellectual consciousness of their spirit, which gives them a curious mind. They use their mental abilities to acquire knowledge, yet their ultimate decisions will not be made by cognitive methods alone.

The ideals they envision can become a moral code for them and a model for justice that they seek to apply in their lives. Willful tantrums can arise suddenly and endure for quite some time. When they connect deeply to their spiritual nature and go beyond the ego's pull, they are able to bring understanding and assistance to others in a more loving and open way.

These souls can be flexible and adapt to a wide variety of environments and settings. In spite of some conflicts and struggles with others, they are balanced within themselves. They are typically attractive and friendships are important to them. Their nature is generous and they may be drawn to some charitable cause, but they are usually able to discern where their gifts will be most appreciated, and just how much to give. They may make decisions fairly quickly, and once they have made up their minds to take some action, they will not delay.

They can be quite family-oriented and enjoy a variety of entertaining pastimes. They are responsive in their relationships with others, although they sometimes feel misunderstood. Their naturally protective nature will likely be heightened if they perceive any threat to those they love. They sometimes need to withdraw into a quieter state and let go of the stress that comes from their acute sensitivity to the words and actions of others. They feel deep compassion for humanity and the natural world, but they need to use caution in regards to drugs, alcohol and other addictive substances, as there may be some tendency to use these things to medicate emotional wounds and soothe their delicate souls.

In any group setting these souls will get along with anyone that they truly respect. In their work, they may not have much tolerance for incompetence, ineptitude or subterfuge, especially among their supervisors. They do better when they can lead and take responsibility for themselves and the project at hand, and are often good at sales, promotion and marketing due to their natural enthusiasm and charm. Their sense of authority and persistent approach to any task assures they will achieve success in anything they undertake. Although they do not take kindly to opposition of any kind, they don't hold grudges once their anger has been expressed, and are able to just move on.

These souls have a great capacity for love, but need to understand that relationships do not operate on their terms alone. Life does not always go according to their carefully crafted plans. Their life lesson is to develop a healthy sense of self-worth, go beyond pride and master humility. But at the same time, if they withdraw too deeply into themselves, they may cut off valuable external input that could lead to wrong decisions. Helping others stimulates their goodwill, and if they focus on service to others they can be true humanitarians. They must also understand that other people can also be of assistance to them.

Their heartfelt desire is to create or contribute to some endeavor that serves the higher good. Whenever they turn the personal will toward spiritual consciousness, they align with the heavens above. Devotion to a spiritual path, philosophy or lifestyle grounds their strong energy, and rewards their steadfastness and tenacity with divine wisdom, love and grace. They look for the good in all people, and need to be careful of those who may take advantage of their charitable nature. Whether they are focused on establishing righteousness and justice for the oppressed, nurturing their loved ones or caring for those in need, these highly independent souls excel when they allow the spirit to lead.

MARCH 11 TO MARCH 20
PERSONALITY PROFILE: 10 OF INTUITION
A Legacy of Success

KEYWORDS

HAPPY SUCCESSFUL AMBITIOUS INTUITIVE IMPULSIVE
COMPASSIONATE MOODY SENSITIVE

These hard-working individuals are likely to gain success in whatever they undertake. Although their achievements may take some time to manifest, they have the tenacity and determination to persist. Their task is to complete karmic patterns from previous incarnations, and establish an enduring legacy on earth. The dynamic nature of their mind and their passionate drive to succeed serve them well in their quest to advance human consciousness and establish a higher life on earth.

They are highly intuitive and may be attracted to metaphysical studies or spiritual life. Even so, they seek to express their spiritual wisdom within the material world. They are inspiring, gracious and harmonious individuals who are usually happy and content. They may feel frustrated at times, because even though they have abundant energy, it remains at a plateau. No additional energy is available to them due to the level of completion that has been attained by the soul. Once they understand this influence, they can more easily overcome feelings of limitation and use these boundaries to creatively focus their intent.

These individuals are naturally in touch with the soul. This provides them with a strong inner direction in every aspect of their lives. Independent, strong-willed and motivated to triumph in life, these capable individuals may experience some difficulty in love. They are committed first and foremost to the accomplishment of their work, and they need a partner who is willing to sacrifice to support them to actualize their dreams.

Their considerable ambition helps them accomplish many things. To others their dedication may seem obsessive or extreme, but these gifted souls are rare on earth and seem to follow the higher will alone. Their acute perceptiveness may give them precognition and prophetic dreams, and they generally act quickly on these inspirations, especially when they show them how to help others and prevent harm. They are little understood by others and this can be painful for them, but they need to realize that they are here to understand others, not to be understood.

Though it may take some time for them to gain success, their attainments are permanent and lasting. When they complete one endeavor or project, they are content to begin again, working on new projects to benefit themselves, their loved ones and humanity. Their material success comes fairly easily, but they are always happy to share. They generally do not seek gain to benefit themselves exclusively, but use it to serve others. Their generous and loving nature often motivates them to make financial contributions to those in need.

Their spiritual mission is demanding and can encompass a great deal of their time. In this regard, they may seem self-focused, selfish or narcissistic. This tendency contributes to the difficulty they find in relationships and family matters. They can become so highly focused upon their higher calling that they may overlook the feelings and needs of others. This can also set them up for deception because they may become too self-absorbed to be fully aware of other peoples' real motivations.

Though they have a natural spiritual awareness, they are equally attracted to the material world. They may sometimes feel pulled in both directions and have difficulty bringing these opposing drives into harmony. When they make up their mind, their strength of will rapidly drives them forward. For better or worse, once they begin, they are bound to complete whatever task they have chosen. Organized and orderly in everything they do, their homes reflect their gentle charm and love of symmetry and beauty.

The greatest lesson they are here to learn is to temper diverse extremes. They need to moderate their love of work with their equal attraction to pleasure. Highly sensual individuals who appreciate physical love, their passion arises from deep within, and their intimate encounters may be impulsive. They are restored and refreshed by spending time in nature. Camping, gardening and hiking are good for their bodies and their souls. Their task in life is to merge the ethereal with the physical, and establish heaven on earth. When they master their volatile, changeable disposition, they may become beneficent leaders and inspirational teachers who leave a lasting legacy of celestial love in terrestrial creation.

Chapter 5

MARCH 21 TO JUNE 20

ARIES, TAURUS, AND GEMINI

SPIRIT TYPE: WORLDLY CONSCIOUSNESS

Manifesting Transcendence

KEYWORDS

INTUITIVE   SENSUAL   EARTHY   CREATIVE   SENSUAL
STUBBORN   CHANGEABLE   FRIENDLY

Those born under the influence of worldly consciousness have a unique affinity for the natural world. Of all the spiritual profiles, these individuals are the most involved with life on earth and all of the endless changes that mark the experience of human manifestation. They provide a grounding presence to those whose lives they touch. Their spiritual destiny involves the conscious integration of spirit and matter, and they are often drawn to study spirituality, particularly anything involving the spiritual powers of the earth itself.

Highly creative, these spirits are interested in creating a family and establishing a home. Their naturally nurturing presence is a source of support for their loved ones. The physical body is of interest to them, whether they are pursuing methods to restore balance and vitality to others, or enjoying sensual indulgences. They are innovators who bring new understandings to light, often related to physical health and well-being.

They have a special interest in physical love and all things that bring bodily pleasure. Their connection to spirit often comes alive in intimate encounters. They need to beware of becoming dependent on external things to awaken their souls, and turn instead to body-centered approaches to enlightenment such as Kundalini and Tantra yoga. In love, they are loyal and protective, and may be distressed by moves, breakups and transitions that bring the loss of loved ones and long-time friends.

These spirits are generally successful at manifesting whatever they need in the world. This indicates a level of completion, and they may find their path filled with many different types of completion. They like to master whatever they undertake to study or perform. In most cases they slowly and methodically explore all aspects of any given discipline or task before moving on to the next course of action. They will maintain their focus until they attain mastery, and when finished, new inspirations and directions arise.

All of nature is their playground, and they are renewed and refreshed whenever they get outdoors. They are drawn to rocks, animals and plants and their work or personal interests may involve any of these. Their energy is highly sensitive and they are receptive to the concerns and emotions of others. For this reason, they need to learn to protect themselves at times and avoid negative environments and people. They do best when they focus on healing, feeding or providing for others.

They can be talented in business and successful in real estate, finance and commerce. They are comfortable in the world of work, and often like to work with their hands, expressing their creativity. They tend to be financially secure, even if they don't have much money. When their needs for security are met by loving relationships, they don't worry much about money. When they are not feeling emotionally secure, they can experience anxiety in relation to their material needs. They are good providers for their families, and when their home life is happy they feel great joy and peace.

When they are aware of and connected to their innermost being, they know there is no separation between the spiritual and material worlds, and they bring this harmonious realization to everyone they meet. They can be pioneers in any field, but may be especially called to advance natural technologies, model sustainable living or be involved in organic farming. They are lovers of animals and some may be found working to preserve and protect wild and exotic animals in their natural habitats. They have an interest in healing plants and herbs, and benefit from the use of them, as well as being a wise guide for others in their use.

These creative and sensitive spirits are generally passive, relaxed and calm. They prefer to handle conflict by stubbornness, withdrawal or 'digging in'. They are slow to anger, but can be explosive when they react, like the volcanoes that lie dormant and then suddenly erupt. Their emotions of hurt, anger or despair may linger longer than for those with other spirit types. They are here to learn how to transmute the ever-changing experiences of life by letting old energies dissolve and building anew.

These tender, loving spirits are friendly and physically attractive. Beyond their connection to the wild, natural earth, they feel at one with the universe itself. They are able to sense and call upon the powers of the planets, stars, sun and moon. Their awakening is stimulated by traditions relating to earth spirituality. If they go deep enough into the power of earth, they may reveal shamanic abilities within themselves. Their perseverance allows them to ultimately become great humanitarians and create a legacy that will endure on earth when they return to the spirit world. They are manifesting their vision of transcendent life on earth by unveiling the earth itself.

MARCH 21 TO APRIL 10
SOUL PROFILE: WILLFUL VISIONARY

KEYWORDS

STRONG-WILLED   COMMANDING   CHARMING   IMPULSIVE
HOT-TEMPERED   CHEERFUL   LOVING   INTUITIVE

The Willful Visionary is a soul with great power. They are often quite determined, but may express this in a passive way. They are motivated by a non-intellectual impulse that gives them an internal feeling of what is best, right and good. All of the Visionary soul types turn the wheel of the universe from one spirit type to the next. The Willful Visionary therefore oversees the last personality profile of the Intellectual consciousness, and the first two personas of the Worldly consciousness.

They have to ensure that their dominant nature does not result in an obsessive need for control. When they feel righteous, they can easily get into difficulty with others. Their motives are innocent however, as they really do want to bring about the highest good. They need to realize that friends and family members have to make their own mistakes and learn from them, and they are not likely to respond favorably to bossiness.

Their strength of will also endows them with great enthusiasm and determination to attain success in life. They are more sensitive and sympathetic than they may at times appear. They receive inspiration from the intellectual consciousness of their spirit, which gives them a curious mind. They use their mental abilities to acquire knowledge, yet their ultimate decisions will not be made by cognitive methods alone.

The ideals they envision can become a moral code for them and a model for justice that they seek to apply in their lives. Willful tantrums can arise suddenly and endure for quite some time. When they connect deeply to their spiritual nature and go beyond the ego's pull, they are able to bring understanding and assistance to others in a more loving and open way.

These souls can be flexible and adapt to a wide variety of environments and settings. In spite of some conflicts and struggles with others, they are balanced within themselves. They are typically attractive and friendships are important to them. Their nature is generous and they may be drawn to some charitable cause, but they are usually able to discern where their gifts will be most appreciated, and just how much to give. They may make decisions fairly quickly, and once they have made up their minds to take some action, they will not delay.

They can be quite family-oriented and enjoy a variety of entertaining pastimes. They are responsive in their relationships with others, although they sometimes feel misunderstood. Their naturally protective nature will likely be heightened if they perceive any threat to those they love. They sometimes need to withdraw into a quieter state and let go of the stress that comes from their acute sensitivity to the words and actions of others. They feel deep compassion for humanity and the natural world, but they need to use caution in regards to drugs, alcohol and other addictive substances, as there may be some tendency to use these things to medicate emotional wounds and soothe their delicate souls.

In any group setting these souls will get along with anyone that they truly respect. In their work, they may not have much tolerance for incompetence, ineptitude or subterfuge, especially among their supervisors. They do better when they can lead and take responsibility for themselves and the project at hand, and are often good at sales, promotion and marketing due to their natural enthusiasm and charm. Their sense of authority and persistent approach to any task assures they will achieve success in anything they undertake. Although they do not take kindly to opposition of any kind, they don't hold grudges once their anger has been expressed, and are able to just move on.

These souls have a great capacity for love, but need to understand that relationships do not operate on their terms alone. Life does not always go according to their carefully crafted plans. Their life lesson is to develop a healthy sense of self-worth, go beyond pride and master humility. But at the same time, if they withdraw too deeply into themselves, they may cut off valuable external input that could lead to wrong decisions. Helping others stimulates their goodwill, and if they focus on service to others they can be true humanitarians. They must also understand that other people can also be of assistance to them.

Their heartfelt desire is to create or contribute to some endeavor that serves the higher good. Whenever they turn the personal will toward spiritual consciousness, they align with the heavens above. Devotion to a spiritual path, philosophy or lifestyle grounds their strong energy, and rewards their steadfastness and tenacity with divine wisdom, love and grace. They look for the good in all people, and need to be careful of those who may take advantage of their charitable nature. Whether they are focused on establishing righteousness and justice for the oppressed, nurturing their loved ones or caring for those in need, these highly independent souls excel when they allow the spirit to lead.

MARCH 21 TO MARCH 30
PERSONALITY PROFILE: 2 OF WILL
Courageous Dominion

KEYWORDS

WILLFUL   AMBITIOUS   ELEGANT   GENEROUS   IMPULSIVE
FIERCE   INDEPENDENT   AGGRESSIVE

Everything these bold individuals do in life is directed from the soul level. Though motivated by spiritual wisdom, they are somewhat prone to conflict due to their impulsive outbursts. They have a noble nature and are willing to fight when necessary to restore peace and harmony. Their efforts to restore order may be overly aggressive as they are naturally domineering individuals. In childhood, they typically face many challenges due to their inner certainty about their soul's direction and spontaneous actions in response to it. They have an intuitive and profound understanding of what is right, which can potentially fuel arguments with others who are not so insightful.

Through these enthusiastic individuals, a synthesis of wisdom and knowledge takes place and abstract concepts take concrete form. They typically make good teachers who are equally adept at complex sciences. The soul lesson for these individuals is discernment. They need to learn that, even though they can often foresee what is best for others, they don't always need to express it in order to convince or command anyone. They must learn to let go of their willful agendas and allow people the freedom to make mistakes, struggle and grow. Their naturally strong-willed ways often result in bossiness and over-control. When they transmute these impulses toward a higher good, they may become wise and beneficent leaders.

They have the ability to acquire detailed information quickly and can interpret intricate theories and make them accessible and clear to others. Due to their unwavering inner certainty, they may appear aloof. Their presence is so powerful that nearly everyone will react to them, for better or worse. Some may feel threatened and react defensively, and this can quickly escalate into tension and potential battles because these individuals are not likely to respond favorably when their authority is questioned. They need to learn that these initial reactions occur due to others' insecurities. When they realize this, they can relax and focus on those who feel reassured within their commanding aura.

These impressive individuals naturally serve as role models for others, whether for good or bad. They can one day master the tremendous power of their personality, provided they consciously commit to practicing humility, surrender and silence in the face of provocation. They have within them a unity of spirit and matter that can help them become equally balanced in giving and receiving. This inner union inspires their high ideals of perfection and desire for their lofty visions to appear in the everyday world. Their inner understandings are from the celestial realm, and are rarely able to manifest on the material plane. They are challenged to let go of ideals of perfection and embrace the often-messy, imperfect world.

They may face challenges in partnerships of all kinds, partly because of their finesse in reconciling and alleviating highly discordant energies and deep incompatibilities. They may go on for too long, trying to balance a volatile relationship, but instead escalating the dynamic by their great force and creating more conflict. They need to learn to transcend their impulses and wait for others to come to them and ask for their assistance, rather than acting proactively on behalf of loved ones or giving specific directions to resolve others' problems or improve their lives. If they remember to turn within when stressed, they can begin to restore order in their surroundings and heal the emotional and karmic wounds that are at the root of their irreconcilable human relationships.

They may sometimes feel misunderstood and isolated from others, and they may well be both. They are here to understand, not to be understood, and to serve others, not to dominate or engage in any personal battle of wills. At the same time, they are natural rulers and leaders who do best when they find careers and interests that can allow their strength to serve a greater good. Their ambition and courage assure them of tremendous success in life; but they ought to make sure that their kingdom is not built on the mistreatment of others or the earth.

They should guard against tendencies to self-medicate their sensitivity with alcohol, food or drugs. These are among the multitude of radical impulses and conquests they may be challenged to transcend. They are here to learn transcendence in every way, and can develop greater self-control and patience through art, music, yoga, meditation, martial arts or long retreats in nature. Being in the natural world helps soothe this fiery soul. They access their spiritual consciousness through spending time outdoors in the meadows, forests, mountains or at the seashore.

MARCH 31 TO APRIL 10
PERSONALITY PROFILE: 3 OF WILL
Charming Fury

KEYWORDS

ENTHUSIASTIC   GENEROUS   LOVING   SELF-FOCUSED
COMMANDING   FAMILY-ORIENTED   OUTSPOKEN
INDEPENDENT

These individuals are typically filled with hope and bring tremendous enthusiasm to the accomplishment of their dreams and goals. They tend to be spiritually oriented and highly intelligent. This combination of interests drives them to appreciate systematic approaches to spirituality, such as organized religions, fraternities or philosophical societies. They have an inherent artistic sensibility, a refined dignity and subtle graciousness. They are gregarious, loving and attractive.

They are highly motivated to do their best in whatever they undertake. They are driven by a strong sense of right and wrong, and may be drawn to fight for justice in many different ways. A combination of strong will and moral righteousness may encourage them to passionately impose their views on others. They are here to learn to live and let live, and to let go of the need to control and command others.

Though they are typically happy and affectionate, they may be prone to moodiness, withdrawal and brooding. Because they are highly sensitive, these brief inner retreats help them regain their emotional balance. They are capable of intense anger when provoked, especially if it involves a perceived threat to their family or loved ones. They are spontaneous and fun loving, but should guard against impulsive indulgences involving money, food, alcohol or drugs.

These spirited individuals are generous and motivated toward charitable works, which they may support with their time and/or their money. They are bold and courageous and do not hesitate to act when prompted by their finely tuned inner certainty. Though they form strong bonds with their life partner, they are highly independent and prefer to take the lead in relationships. They typically play a leadership role in family dynamics as well.

Their natural air of command is reassuring for those seeking protection and security. They can also be perceived as a threatening presence by those who are not receptive to the power of their dominion. They may act or react recklessly, without sufficient thought or contemplation, when they are provoked. They are exceedingly forthright and outspoken, leaving others with no uncertainty as to their true, heartfelt opinions. One of their life challenges is to learn to ground themselves and sit still when their fiery temperament is aroused.

These individuals can inspire others to do their best and succeed in attaining their dreams. They often have an affinity for physical activity, music, writing and entertaining. They do best when they find outlets for their abundant creative energy. They are hard workers and devoted partners and parents who need to be recognized for the sensitive and encouraging individuals they truly are. Though they may vent their displeasure and anger forcefully, their fury rarely endures for long before their innate cheerfulness and joy returns.

These self-focused individuals are adept at organizing and supervising others. They can be relied upon to complete tasks efficiently and willingly. Their enthusiasm is contagious and their good humor is endearing. When they learn to tame their passions and detach from the details, they can serve as inspirational leaders and life-long, loyal friends. As they mature they can come into their own as philanthropists, humanitarians and promoters of the highest good. They are here to activate the higher virtues within people and shower goodness upon the earth.

APRIL 11 TO MAY 10
SOUL PROFILE: WORLDLY MEDIATOR

KEYWORDS

CREATIVE   EARTHY   NATURAL   FRIENDLY   SENSUAL
STUBBORN   PATIENT   HARD-WORKING

These innovative souls are most at home in the center of it all. They work hard and have tremendous enthusiasm for everything they do. They are masters of change and move between cycles of intense activity and profound rest. When they are inspired, they become energized and seek many diverse ways to create and share with others. They are cooperative and friendly, and are typically involved in many inventive endeavors at once. While very good at mediating conflicts, they generally prefer to avoid them.

These individuals can be quite engaging and have a laid-back approach to life. Still, like all Mediators, they are often surrounded by calendars, date books, organizers and records of all kinds to help them keep track of their work, social and family engagements. They enjoy bringing people together to learn, celebrate and exchange information.

Very intelligent, they seek knowledge that will help them express their avant-garde awareness in definite material ways. They prefer to go deeply into any course of study they undertake, completely mastering it before moving on. They patiently examine all aspects of any philosophy or theory, finding cutting-edge ways to synthesize science and wisdom in service to a better world.

These souls have a particular affinity for the earth and all things related to natural life. They may be involved in occupations related to the environment, organic foods, healing plants, gardening and farming. They are good at balancing technology and art, allowing them to awaken others in dramatic and entertaining ways. They are adventurous and love to travel the world, meeting new people and learning by immersion into foreign cultures. Their carefree and tolerant nature helps them feel at home wherever they may be.

These gentle souls are primarily passive and prefer peace at all costs. They have a generally stable emotional nature and are loyal and reliable friends. Though they are slow to anger, when they finally reach their limit, rage may well erupt. They tend to focus on their intentions in a quiet and patient way, slowly cultivating their vision of heaven on earth. Like all of the Mediator soul types, they engage in assisting others through mediation, conflict resolution and balancing delicate dynamics. They are aware of the flow of energy between the spiritual and earthly planes, and use their intuition in the service of harmony and peace.

They are typically quite curious and have a desire to learn about many things. Their approach is easy-going and they don't do well with stress. Because they are almost always busy, it is important for them to remember to take time out and retreat. Being immersed in nature – camping, hiking or swimming – restores their vital energy and recharges this active soul. They strive to find the middle ground in most circumstances, but need to guard against tendencies to persist in finding equitable solutions where none may actually exist.

These souls shift from engagement with a very hectic life into more subdued periods of deep relaxation and rest. When their energy drops, they enthusiastically pursue a much needed and lengthy break. They can become a little lazy and slothful at times, and may need to guard against idleness and over-indulgence because they very much enjoy physical and sensual pleasures. They tend to muse upon an abundance of creative ideas that flow endlessly through their minds. When their inspiration crests, they return to the world to manifest their new-found designs.

In relationships they are charming, and love their family and friends. Although they may journey far from home, they always miss their loved ones and are anxious to see them when they return. They are highly sensitive and intuitive, and should take precautions to avoid picking up negative energies from others. When they find imaginative ways to express the great harmony they sense between spiritual truth and material life, they wholeheartedly commit to the accomplishment of the greater mission of the soul.

APRIL 11 TO APRIL 20
PERSONALITY PROFILE: 4 OF WILL
Courageous Love

KEYWORDS

LOVING   KIND   IMPULSIVE   ORDERLY   WILLFUL
EMOTIONAL   COURAGEOUS   CLEVER

These quiet, loving people have a deep desire to assist and benefit others. They balance a tenacious will with gentleness, kindness and grace. In love, they typically direct this willful tendency to be of service to their partner and children, and alternate between passivity and strength. This means they may not speak up when provoked, but instead harbor their feelings until they suddenly explode in anger. Their life lesson involves mastering the ability to speak their truth, while letting go of fears that may cause them to suppress feelings and reactions.

Their desire to help people is so strong that they may develop co-dependencies with those who are unbalanced by emotional turmoil, mental stress or alcohol and drug abuse. They are generally orderly in their lives and habits, and appreciate the rhythms and cycles of life. They are charismatic and endearing, but they can be stubborn when they want to get their way. They have a tendency to be emotionally over-controlled and can benefit from opportunities to express themselves deeply and fully.

These individuals are typically receptive, visionary and intuitive. They are spiritually aware and are often drawn toward metaphysical and mystical studies, as they carry an inner vision of a more perfect and loving world. This motivates great compassion within them and drives their generosity toward others. They know deep down that their vision is reasonable and strive to improve the world while being of service to humanity.

They are natural caretakers, but don't always discern who is ready to benefit from their guidance and support. They may feel frustrated when their advice is ignored. They don't always set proper limits and boundaries, and may be taken advantage of in relationships. They are susceptible to manipulation due to their desire to avoid conflict. Their intuition can help them stay on track and see others' motives more clearly, but they must consciously remember to listen to their inner voice before acting impulsively, and potentially setting themselves up to be betrayed.

These clever people have a delightful sense of humor that helps them greatly in life. They are diligent workers who gain success by finding and following their spiritual calling and can make excellent counselors, advisors and guides. They may also do well in healing professions including spiritual or psychic healing. They seek out knowledge in a variety of disciplines before settling into a focused course of study.

Their spontaneity and instinctive reactions often direct their love life as well, prompting them to leap into relationships before establishing a sufficient foundation. Their hearts can be quickly captivated and they sometimes end up making serious commitments before they have had time to really get to know their partner or mate. They are typically traditional in their views and will prefer to marry those with whom they fall in love. While the fire of their love bursts suddenly into a blaze, they may regret their precipitous decisions as time goes on and more is revealed about their intimate other.

For all of their fiery passion, these individuals are very sensitive and can be easily hurt. They may withdraw and resign, feeling victimized by the world. Isolated, and with only their intuition to guide them, they may surrender too soon when challenged, rather than persisting and claiming their rights. This is the primary karma that they have come to transmute. Imbalanced relationships represent past life lessons that they must complete. When they learn to persevere and insist on receiving no less than what they give to others, the soul grows in wisdom and old wounds are healed.

They are reasonable and reliable in whatever they undertake. They take their responsibilities seriously and accomplish tasks efficiently. They ultimately finish whatever they begin, but they usually take several breaks along the way. They are able to view all perspectives and discern a balanced approach. As they mature, they awaken to knowledge they have attained in previous incarnations, and can apply this knowledge to help them master the art of turning high ideals into great works on earth.

These energetic, gracious individuals encounter good fortune in life as a reward for their past lives of service to others. They are a blessing to their loved ones and friends, due to their loyalty and generosity. Though they might struggle with challenges in financial and material life, their soul's loving nature ensures that they are protected and provided for in remarkable ways, often when least expected. They gain strength from tempering their feisty nature, which increases their wisdom and goodwill. When they master the power of their inspired ambition, their heartfelt intentions come to fruition and victory is assured.

APRIL 21 TO 30
PERSONALITY PROFILE: 5 OF WORLD
Revolutionary Reconstruction

KEYWORDS

KIND   CREATIVE   WILLFUL   INNOVATIVE   TALKATIVE
IMPULSIVE   ANXIOUS   LOVING

These progressive individuals can bring radical changes to life on earth. Their curiosity draws them toward the natural world and stimulates travel. They have the potential for great success, but their journey to the goal may be burdened by changes, endings and disruptions. Engaging and talkative, people are attracted by their kindness and charm. They may be quite psychic or visionary and can apply these gifts to help others and the world.

They can gain success in any endeavor involving the public, such as marketing or promotion. They may direct their efforts in ways that can advance human knowledge of nature's healing powers, the interconnectedness of life on earth, and the sacredness of cultural and ecological diversity. Some of them spend time exploring the world nomadically, enriching the soul by learning from life itself. They have a somewhat mystical nature, which subtly guides their most important actions. Whether they are involved with loved ones at home or living in foreign lands, they can rely upon their soul connection to give them steady peace in the midst of any uncertainty.

When they are young, they may feel some sadness that is likely the remnant of unresolved emotions they have brought with them from their immediate past life. They may suffer some personal losses, which can lead them to develop a fear of commitment in intimate relationships. It can also stimulate their natural independence, which they may fiercely cling to in the presence of significant others. As they grow, they learn to let go and transcend the past. Once they are freed from these emotional burdens, they are likely to be blessed with a loving and enduring relationship.

They have the potential for financial success because they are able to intuit which endeavors will increase their wealth quickly. They work diligently toward their goals, but having reached them, they may well abandon a successful enterprise if they feel called to move on to the next inspiration. They passionately invest their time and attention into all of their creative works and must guard against workaholic tendencies, stress and strain. Due to their inherent drive and determination, they typically do better when they take ownership of their own business, organization or profession.

They are prone to worry and indecision, and must try to develop their faith. They may be somewhat wary and distrustful, which should be turned toward healthy skepticism or it can spiral downward into misgivings and doubt. They are good at keeping secrets and value their privacy. They protect their family and loved ones with a tenacious and stubborn reserve.

Later in life they may develop an interest in spiritual studies or metaphysical pursuits. This is an important resource that can bring them greater peace. They may benefit from working with a spiritual teacher or mentor. These disciplines help them attain a more consistent connection to the soul. Spiritual study provides an opportunity to find the answers to persistent questions they have regarding the subtle energies and memories that surround them. Learning the nature of universal influences such as astrology can help them master deep-seated anxieties and gain confidence in an ever-changing world.

These individuals have tremendous power and a strong will to succeed in every area of life. They witness the rise and demise of many things around them – people, relationships, jobs, environments, and so on. They do not experience life as one complete book. For them it is more like a collection of short stories, each one reflecting a beginning, middle and end.

Their special spiritual powers can only be accessed when they turn their attention within. Their challenge is to learn to distinguish their unmet inner needs from their true spiritual goals and dreams. Likewise, when they step back from outer world demands, they are able to manifest their own inner truth. They are here to heal from past soul traumas, and by doing so, a profound metamorphosis can take place.

It is important for these individuals to realize that nothing is ever lost, only endlessly transformed. When they go with the flow without attachment, they gain the freedom to be themselves. They need to realize the paradoxical reality that every act of creation necessarily involves destruction. By skillfully dispersing universal energies, they carve out the leading edge in inspired and ingenious ways. They are mastering the power of change to redefine themselves and revolutionize the world.

MAY 1 TO MAY 10
PERSONALITY PROFILE: 6 OF WORLD
Creative Success

KEYWORDS

| COOPERATIVE | SENSUOUS | PROSPEROUS | CREATIVE |
| GENEROUS | SENSITIVE | MOODY | STUBBORN |

These charismatic individuals can experience considerable success in worldly and spiritual endeavors. They are generally content and peaceful, and enthusiastic at work and play. They are nurturers who love to express their kindness and concern for family and friends alike. Natural team players, they enjoy tasks and projects that require practical organization, and are methodical and persistent in accomplishing all things. They take their time to thoroughly master knowledge in one arena before moving on to other subjects.

They are consistently in touch with the soul and oriented toward faith. Their boundless energy is engaging and they can charm their way into anyone's heart. While they enjoy relaxation, especially in nature, they should limit indulgences in inertia and laziness, which they can also quite enjoy. They maintain a childlike innocence and belief in the goodness of humankind, and are helpful mediators who can find realistic and constructive solutions to conflict of all kinds. Their giving heart and tenacious approach may tempt them to persevere too long, and they need to be willing to wind down negotiations when it becomes apparent that defeat may be inevitable. However, they can take comfort that their many successes will offset the occasional loss.

They can apply an innate stubbornness as a way of establishing their will, and are likely to dig in for quite some time when they want to get their way. They likewise hold on to what they hold dear, such as family, friends and possessions. Because they are sensitive and receptive, they can also pick up distressing emotions and moods from other people. They need to remember to let these things go because they don't actually belong to them. Their own emotional hurts and moods may linger for a long time as well. Rather than going into a rage, they may sulk, lament and pout. As they mature, they learn to adapt to the imperfections and slights of the world, and remember to love themselves and move on.

These warm-hearted individuals draw their strength from the physical energy of the earth. Their sensuality and sexuality are experienced in their true spiritual state. They are physically loving, cuddly and affectionate because they experience all of life in a tangible way. They are especially skillful at merging the spiritual into intimate realms. They appreciate a partner who shares their love of nature and all outdoor activities. They provide a grounding influence to their children and mates. Generous and willing to share their time and money, they often help provide for those in need.

Because they delight in bodily pleasure, they need to guard against over-indulgence in alcohol, drugs and food. They are generally steady and good with their hands. In spite of their overall tranquility, they can almost always be counted on to bring exuberant energy toward the improvement of the wellbeing of others and the health of the planet. They have an affinity for hands-on healing, medicinal herbs and natural remedies drawn from the earth. Their spiritual powers are activated in nature and they do best when they spend considerable time enjoying the outdoors.

They often gain positions of power, giving them wide influence over others. They are here to initiate great changes in the world. Their adaptability and cooperative manner contribute to their popularity and achievements. They are often financially successful, prosperous or wealthy. Their passions run deep and they do not usually engage in any superficiality, but have keen insights and strong intuitions that come from their alignment with the soul. These visions lead them to discover new resources to meet human needs and apply to the accomplishment of their spiritual mission as well.

These gentle individuals are in tune with the rhythms of the earth and the universe. They should realize the value of downtime, when they can integrate all they have learned. They are compassionate and their empathy is so acute that they may actually feel the feelings of others. Their tender heart prompts them to assist humanity in constructive and innovative ways, and they are likely to receive gratitude and love throughout their lives. They carry a subtle personal power that allows them to be fully present in a definite, physical way. Their mission involves the reconciliation of heaven and earth, and the more they complete this blending within themselves, the better they can guide and bless others with their radiant presence and spiritual wisdom.

MAY 11 TO JUNE 10
SOUL PROFILE: INTELLECTUAL WARRIOR

KEYWORDS

INTELLECTUAL ACTIVE CLEVER COURAGEOUS SENSITIVE
INTENSE CREATIVE INSPIRED HEADSTRONG

These experienced, old souls bring higher ideals and inspiration into the world. They have a deep connection to great wisdom, but they find it difficult to put this into words. The abstract knowledge they are born with makes it impossible for them to have much interest in superficial opinions based on shallow or incomplete understandings. They feel attracted to both spiritual and material life, and it may take them some time to reconcile these desires. Their highly intelligent nature prompts them to study a variety of academic disciplines; however, they may not stick to one particular field for long as their interests are subject to change. Their minds are highly active and their thought processes are generally clear and refined.

The wide variety of studies they engage in stimulates their inquisitive mind and enables them to master complex systems that encompass the lofty values they embrace. While their intellectual abilities are very great, their excessive mental activity can lead to tension and fatigue. Whatever useful information they receive, they readily give to others. Because of this ability, they may serve as teachers, counselors, activists or humanitarians. They enjoy books, libraries and the Internet, which provide them with rich resources to master and share.

These souls need to learn to balance physical activity and mental work. When they get out in nature they are able to get the mind out of the way. All physical activities are beneficial for them including dance, yoga and even shamanic arts. The earth is their natural healer, restoring their energy and nurturing the soul. They need to become more connected to the emotional part of life and not be so constantly caught up in intellectual drives.

They have a commanding presence and do better in situations where their natural leadership abilities are appreciated. While many people feel safe and protected in their presence, others may feel threatened by them, without them ever speaking a word. It is important for these souls to recognize that this reaction has nothing to do with them, and there's really no need to fight back. When they allow themselves to simply avoid those who fear them, they come into their own and shine. They are typically independent, but can work well with others for a time. In the end they may choose a career and lifestyle that allows them to be their own boss.

As these souls are highly creative, they express themselves in many ways. Painting, sculpture, music and photography allow them to bring out their deeper wisdom, which is transcendent of language and better represented by symbolic forms. In love they are sweet, sensitive and natural romantics. They need a life partner who appreciates their inward musings, but can equally stimulate their fun-loving side. They are generally very close to their family members and devoted to lifelong friends. Their graceful presence and charming manner are endearing, and they are often physically attractive.

Their strong determination and ability to focus intensely on whatever they desire can lead to great success in spite of some battles along the way. As Warriors they are tenacious and self-focused, aiming their great power toward the accomplishment of their goals. They create a magnetic energy field that attracts attention for good or for bad. They prefer not to engage in strife, but can be stubborn when it comes to getting their own way. When their interest is drawn toward something they desperately want, they will easily ignore the input of others as they dive into their quest. Their loved ones are well advised to allow them free reign whenever their abundant energy drives them where others may fear to tread.

These souls have access to ethereal wisdom and they spend a great deal of time acquiring information that validates what they already know. Though they are not particularly organized in their approach to learning, they intuitively understand the intricacies of complex systems. Ultimately, they may formulate new outlets for existing knowledge and create innovative approaches that improve the world. They inspire everyone they meet with their gregarious nature and their gifted awareness of the deeper mysteries of life.

In the midst of so many spontaneous inspirations and insights, these Warriors need to focus on each important mission in life. As they mature, this quest comes into focus more clearly. They have come to inform and inspire others, and to master life's challenges and difficulties along the way. They receive and give loving wisdom in enchanting and entertaining ways. They do best when they can teach, heal or lead others using practical and tangible methods. When they take up their spiritual mission, they bring a heavenly light into everyday life on earth.

MAY 11 TO MAY 20
PERSONALITY PROFILE: 7 OF WORLD
Integral Inspiration

KEYWORDS

CHARMING   INTELLIGENT   CREATIVE   LOVING   STUBBORN
IMPATIENT   PERSISTENT   SENSUOUS

These individuals are highly intuitive and may experience precognitions or prophetic dreams. Powerful spiritual energy forms an intimate connection within the cells of their bodies – they could be said to feel their way through life under this ever-present influence. Their mystical tendencies are especially drawn out by nature and the natural world. They are sensual and earthy, preferring a hands-on approach to learning, work and life. They are sweet natured in general and highly sensitive. If injured emotionally in childhood, it can take them many years to recover and trust again.

These creative and artistic individuals are enthusiastic and full of energy. They are equally capable of great concentration when their attention becomes immersed in any passionate interest. They are highly intelligent and have a love of education, provided it encompasses an experiential approach. Their emotions can be chaotic at times due to their receptive nature. They need time to process acute reactions, and may require support to bring some reasoning to bear and help restore balance.

They are sharp-witted and observant comedians, who love to laugh and bring joy to others. They prefer unconventional methods and unstructured means. They are aware of the vibrations of speech, regardless of the words spoken, and can sense the true intentions of those with whom they interact. Their life is at heart an artistic expression of subtle ideals of beauty and truth.

They need outlets for their abundant imagination and should cultivate time devoted to their artistic instincts. They have many desires, but are challenged to see them through to completion in an orderly way. When their ideals do manifest, they may find they do not always endure. Their victory lies in the process rather than in the results. These individuals can succeed in a range of endeavors. They typically find scientific validation for their inner, mystical understanding, which may stimulate them to be of service to others by teaching, coaching or advising.

The personal energy of these individuals is complementary to the soul. Their strong mind is a gift from the soul, and the personality is able to express its knowledge on the material plane in incredibly innovative ways. These individuals need to remember to have faith, and to wait and see what comes from their hard work. Their strength is not in establishing enduring forms, but in demonstrating the power of passion to motivate earthly life. They may feel pulled in several directions as they learn to synthesize physical pleasures with the elevated ideals of the soul.

They receive accurate inspiration from the soul, but may not always act on it due to their blissful captivation with the material world. They are not always able to logically explain their motives and actions. Their mind operates beyond logic and they are moved only by their inner visceral impulses. They are supportive listeners who can give good advice. Their tendency to give their love freely to others means that they must be cautious to avoid those who would take advantage of them, and learn to discern who to trust with their delicate heart.

Though they are filled with tremendous compassion, they are not always strong enough to set proper limits. They may at times use stubborn withdrawal to get what they want. They are lovers, not fighters, though they are here to learn that it is okay to fight for what they believe. At times, they may feel depleted and in need of a good long rest. They are refreshed by the earth when they spend time outdoors, gardening, camping and hiking in nature.

They may experience frustration and feel limited by circumstances as they begin to establish themselves. These struggles represent a testing of their faith and an initiatory process that will awaken greater wisdom. They appreciate familiar environments, loved ones and life-long friends, preferring to stay with what is familiar to provide a secure foundation they can return to as they begin to explore the world. They are patient and persistent, and confident that good fortune will come their way. Generally resourceful, they can be intensely serious when their curiosity is inflamed.

These individuals teach others to reimagine their own values to encourage free and natural life. Their single-minded potential allows them to master whatever they undertake. They grow in spiritual strength and wisdom as they mature, but seldom lose their youthful exuberance regardless of their age. Their keen intelligence and tender, loving ways are magnetic and their charisma is boundless. They are masters of creation who radiate divine intentions on earth. They come to this life with a mission to encourage happier, healthier life on earth, and share their magical talismans of grace, laughter and good will wholeheartedly and sincerely with those whose lives they touch.

MAY 21 TO MAY 31
PERSONALITY PROFILE: 8 OF INTELLECT
Cherished Beliefs

KEYWORDS

INTELLECTUAL   SOCIABLE   WITTY   ROMANTIC
CHANGEABLE   PATIENT   GENEROUS   IMPULSIVE   MOODY

These individuals have plenty of mental energy available to satisfy their expansive curiosity. They are very social and enjoy gatherings, engagements and outings with their many friends. Knowledgeable on many topics, they enjoy sharing their expertise with others. They are typically rational and logical, which may make it difficult for them to experience feelings and emotions, which are chaotic and irrational. They have diverse interests and tend to split their attention between them, rather than focus on one at a time. Once they form an opinion, they hold onto their beliefs tenaciously, even though these ideas may no longer be serving their own best interests.

They enjoy socializing and environments that facilitate an exchange of ideas. They can be excellent teachers, if they can be persuaded to focus long enough to complete their academic training. When they do narrow in on one chosen field, they are able to quickly analyze and categorize concepts and principle. This is because their knowledge base is broad and encompasses a variety of topics. They can be witty and entertaining speakers and excel in all tasks requiring superior writing or communication skills.

These energetic individuals are good at weaving people together through social groups, in work environments and within the family. It helps their soul growth to focus on being a blessing to others, including sometimes taking positions of authority for the sake of others. They can receive recognition and success in whatever they undertake. However, they are here to learn to be responsible and more aware of the impact of the *instant karma* that can come their way, especially in light of the metaphysical principle, *what we believe, we receive*. With so much inspiration arising in their minds, they are wise to slow down and contemplate further before adopting any belief.

Their adventurous and curious nature may prompt them to travel and explore. They appreciate cultural diversity, unless they received unfavorable messages in their childhood environment. Whenever rigid beliefs have set in, they need to be aware and take up the courage to align with the soul to throw off errors and misunderstandings. They don't always have the strength to stand up for themselves in family affairs or in love, and may suppress powerful feelings for long periods of time and explode when they can no longer endure the pressure.

They are natural romantics, and when they find real love, they contribute stability to their relationships. They may feel misunderstood at times and separate from the soul. The soul has pure wisdom and can provide them with an understanding that lies beyond words, once they have surrendered lower ideas. It helps them to experience the natural chaos of the body that passion and sensuality unleash. A core challenge is to master these powers of the body and find ways to use them to go beyond the mind.

They must discern when obstacles are arising because of their cherished beliefs. They need to let go of these entrenched values and become willing to experience the unfamiliar and unknown. They tend to be emotional in an intellectual way, thinking about their feelings rather than feeling them. The solution is to get out in nature and interact with the earth. Their spiritual nature is worldly and when they are outdoors, they receive blessings of harmony, peace and healing. They should avoid temptations to use their intellectual gifts to try to impose their preferences on others.

These generous individuals are patient and diligent in making their dreams come true. They hold a vision of a more perfect world and respond to the goodness in all. They typically support a variety of charitable causes and can benefit from fine-tuning their philanthropy to allow one project to grow before turning in new directions. Their personal style may be somewhat disorderly, as they tend to get caught up in the minor details at the expense of the primary goal. Their interests and hearts continually expand and they are a blessing to many in life.

Their keynote for life is liberation. They gain stronger contact with the soul when they unchain themselves from self-imposed limitations. Their life lesson is to realize that disruption and discontinuity can empower a superior kind of strength. A great store of truth and beauty come through them when their liberation is attained. Their soul mission in life is to gain harmony, love and serenity from within and share with others in a spirit of spontaneous beneficence. Their quest is well supported by the use of visual meditation techniques, which effectively harness and redirect the energy of their powerful minds.

JUNE 1 TO JUNE 10
PERSONALITY PROFILE: 9 OF INTELLECT
Faithful Transcendence

KEYWORDS

INTELLIGENT	SENSUAL	IMAGINATIVE	CHANGEABLE
MOODY	CONFLICTED	PATIENT	FAITHFUL

It is a blessing that these individuals have a natural and instinctive faith. This allows them to thrive in the midst of life's challenges and end past karma completely. They often come into this life with memories of cruelty from a past life. Themes of oppression may repeat or replay in various ways in this lifetime. Their good humor and optimism help them survive and they will generally succeed in spite of these trials.

Alternatively, they may be guilty of abuse or exploitation themselves. In this case they need to be willing to get help to undo the negative consequences of their own past mistreatment instead of taking it out on others. This theme of healing the lingering effects of injustice can have great impact on their personal relationships and family life. Once they realize that this core challenge exists for the sake of completion, they can more easily touch the pain of the past and allow it to be resolved and released. They must guard against using the mind as a strategy to avoid these sensitive emotions and become willing to surrender to the process.

They are highly intelligent and generally thoughtful, though their opinions are subject to change. They need outlets for their vast creativity, or they may turn to worry and doubt. They are often visionary and intuitive, and may even have some psychic gifts such as precognition and prophetic dreams. They are sometimes aware of the invisible realms and in touch with spiritual guides and loved ones who have passed on.

Their strong sexual energy may complicate the oppressive weight of the soul injuries that need healing; making it likely they may experience some betrayal or betray others themselves. While they may not feel much trust early in life, their challenge is to learn to wisely discern who they can really trust. They may have spontaneous emotional outbursts, which can lead to despair, but they must work to build their tolerance to tender feelings and cope with their volatile emotions. As they mature and heal their wounds, they can let their suspicions go. Once they are freed from the burdens of the past, they can inspire others to recover and grow.

Fiery spiritual energy flows in their blood and gets expressed in good times and bad. These strong-willed individuals can be ruthless when determined to get their way. Aggressive and argumentative when provoked, they may be impatient, intolerant or unkind. However, they can transmute suffering into transcendence with this same dynamic force. When they learn to channel their great power into creative works, political leadership or professional sports, they can gain recognition and fame.

They can prosper in a variety of careers and do best when they focus on work that takes advantage of their natural leadership skills. They can make good teachers provided they learn to tolerate limitations. In team settings they can be counted upon to express their opinions and share their point of view with little encouragement. As they mature they may find they prefer to work independently where they can more freely act on their instincts and find ways to apply their relentless energy toward greater financial achievements.

These individuals are ambitious and entertaining. They are generally physically healthy and may enjoy athletics, exercise and competitive games. They are good communicators with a superior memory. Typical life lessons include mastering concentration and learning to see things through to completion. It is possible for them to transmute their stubborn tendencies into a determined persistence that will bring them great rewards.

They benefit from developing a philosophy of life, which inspires them to turn their willpower toward good works. They are aware of the struggles and errors of humanity, which can motivate them to help alleviate suffering and strife. They are sometimes drawn to spiritual life, finding useful disciplines to take them beyond the mind. These approaches are ideal for the growth of the soul, which needs to let go of regrets and revenge. They need to release their nightmares in order to discover new dreams. As love for themselves awakens and grows, their compassion is activated to a higher degree. Their faith serves them well through life's ups and downs, and their perseverance is often rewarded with spectacular and lasting results.

JUNE 11 TO JUNE 20
SOUL PROFILE: INTUITIVE VISIONARY

KEYWORDS

MYSTICAL   SENSITIVE   WISE   COMPASSIONATE   SPIRITUAL
NURTURING   EMPATHIC   EMOTIONAL

This soul's energy is derived from the feminine source, and is very nurturing, giving and creative. They are compassionate, concerned for others and focused on family. These souls tend to be organized, and create a sense of order in their environments. They like to keep everyone harmonious and happy. All of the Visionary soul types turn the wheel of the universe from one spirit type to the next. The Intuitive Visionary therefore oversees the last personality profile of the Worldly consciousness, and the first two personas of the Willful consciousness.

Their profound depth and understanding makes them not only sympathetic but acutely empathic. They tend to absorb feelings and energy from others and from their environment, and reflect it back to those around them. It is important for them to master this potentially healing gift, and not be disempowered by caretaking others or taking on too much negative energy.

Emotional, moody and very intense, the fire of willful consciousness illuminates these paradoxically placid souls, and gives them a strong psychic nature. They not only have deep knowledge, but are gifted with being able to explain the essence of this wisdom to others. They like to organize information and often learn or create systems that further human understanding. These souls are very interested in helping others in a wide variety of ways, including feeding, comforting, housing, nurturing, giving wisdom, inspiring, harmonizing and clarifying.

These individuals do best when they create ways to share their spiritual faith, heartfelt impressions, and intuitions with others in life. When the Intuitive Visionary sets out to assist others, they do so in a way that brings forth whatever may be lying beneath the surface, waiting to be seen and healed. These souls bring unique spiritual gifts to a world in which they are desperately needed; however, they often feel distant from the material world and more at home on the inner planes.

They carry a deep wisdom that manifests in unusual ways and they need to find outlets for their innovative understandings. They may feel isolated and misunderstood, which is very real because few can understand the mysterious ways of the Visionary soul. They can be passive at times, especially in relationships and they must learn to develop a stronger will to prevent others from taking advantage of them. They are highly receptive and easily pick up prevailing forces and passions from environments and people. They need to remember to consciously release these things in order to preserve their serenity and peace of mind.

They are highly compassionate and often seek ways to help improve the world. Their great sensitivity causes them to react strongly to the words and actions of others. Their memory is particular enduring and it takes a long time for them to forget wounding words. They not only hold onto the past, but to people and things as well, and are particularly fond of bowls, vases, boxes and bags, which symbolize containment.

Like all of the Visionaries, they are commanding and can easily oversee large projects, family matters and projects of all kinds. They are good at directing and encouraging the successful completion of any task because they see the big picture as well as intuiting the best application of the skills of each person involved. They need to be careful that their masterful oversight doesn't devolve into bossiness or control. They are here to learn to perfect the delicate balance between encouragement and dominion.

These souls are natural clairvoyants and rely upon their strong inner connections to guide them in life. If they choose to do so, they may be successful as spiritual advisors. At the least they will serve their family and friends with accurate insights and guidance. Their dreams may be precognitive and prophetic, and they may be aware of the invisible beings who are always present in the world. As children this can be difficult because they are typically unaware that not everyone shares this spiritual gift. As they mature, the resources they find to support their spiritual nature can range from charismatic churches to ritual lodges. One way or another they will be drawn to prayer, meditation and spiritual life.

These insightful individuals can be successful in a variety of ways. Counseling, creating or teaching are some of the outlets that can sustain them. In love they are tender, sensitive and sensual and they need a partner who appreciates their magical ways. As parents they are nurturing and committed to meeting their children's needs. They need to be careful of over-involvement and avoid smothering their loved ones by becoming entangled in their lives. When they learn to step back and allow others to learn from their struggles, they complete one of the most important goals of the soul.

The qualities of the Intuitive Visionary are absorbent, reflective and changeable, stimulating sensitivity, insight and healing for humankind. They are imaginative, creative, kind, nurturing and mystical. They are strong spiritual leaders once they have mastered their sensitive nature, and can benefit others by exposing them to the reality of the unseen, inner and spiritual aspects of life.

JUNE 11 TO JUNE 20
PERSONALITY PROFILE: 10 OF INTELLECT
Commanding Insight

KEYWORDS

ADAPTABLE   FRIENDLY   INTUITIVE   SENSITIVE
COMMUNICATIVE   ARGUMENTATIVE   INTELLIGENT   MOODY

These individuals are typically friendly and outgoing with a good sense of humor. They are quick-minded, but deeply reflective. Sensitive to the words and actions of others, they may hold onto hurt feelings for quite some time. They are often born with some emotional despair brought forward from their immediate past life. Present life turmoil may sometimes follow, presenting opportunities to let go, heal and transcend. They have incarnated to complete karma, learn profound spiritual lessons and master psychic and clairvoyant gifts.

Endings and completion are recurring themes in their lives. They often must cope with grief and sorrow early in life, as the unexpressed emotions from their previous incarnation are released. They must guard against resignation, depression and discouragement. Their heartfelt faith can sustain and comfort them through these difficulties, and they need to remember that these events mark the completion of old patterns, relationships and attitudes. Their life lesson is to let go and embrace the joy of new beginnings.

Though they are efficient and reliable in their careers, they may be disorganized in their personal life and home environment. They are talkative and enjoy getting together with friends; however, they need to avoid the tendency to engage in gossip. They are loyal and helpful friends whose exceeding kindness may leave them open them to manipulation or exploitation. When they find themselves in unbalanced relationships, they need to be aware that karma is in play. As they give up involvement in destructive relationships, their karma is completed, which frees them to grow in wisdom and love.

In most cases, these individuals are able to continue to re-establish a positive attitude in spite of the challenges they face. They are naturally adaptable and flexible, and mostly willing to keep an open mind. Lovers of nature and all things of the earth, outdoors stimulates their spiritual energy and connects them to the soul. Spending time in nature helps them recover from stress and tension by giving the active mind a rest. They enjoy gardening, camping and swimming, and benefit from nature retreats.

They are good communicators who can explain detailed information clearly. They crave a variety of mental stimulation, but need to learn to persevere in one direction until mastery is attained. They should refrain from speaking until they take time to carefully consider and screen their thoughts. Otherwise their impulsive responses may lead them to regret their own words. They need to take time to inwardly reflect in order to quiet the mind. Meditation is beneficial to them because it opens them to the wisdom they hold inside.

These individuals have a powerful presence, even though they are primarily easygoing. They should attempt to become more aware of the potent effect they can have on other people. With their sharp command of words, they may be too quick to criticize others. Even when they are relaxed, there is an air of command that surrounds them. Those in need of protection or love will feel reassured by their presence. Those who react to power with fear may verbally attack them for no apparent reason. When they realize that this reaction reflects the insecurity of others, they can avoid arguments and simply avoid contact with those who are uncomfortable in their presence.

They tend toward dependency in relationships, which highlights their life challenge to attain greater autonomy. They are loving and generous, and don't always stand up for themselves when they should. Highly sensual, they need a partner who can match their abundant physical energy. They have in mind the best interests of others, yet their good intentions can go overboard and feel controlling to their loved ones and friends.

These individuals can be very serious in their contemplation of life. They are gentle humanitarians who want to support an evolution of consciousness on earth. Because of this they can be good counselors, teachers and guides, and have a special affinity for spiritual healing should they choose to pursue that path. If they concentrate their abundant energy toward any goal that allows them to be of service to others, they are certain to succeed. They are capable of a good deal of spiritual power and insight, which can stimulate their personal growth and the development of the soul. As they mature, they develop a better understanding of how and when they can apply this dynamic awareness to help those who can most benefit from their acute perceptions and down-to-earth advice.

www.ingramcontent.com/pod-product-compliance
Lightning Source LLC
Chambersburg PA
CBHW070617300426
44113CB00010B/1559